Communications
in Computer and Information Science   1351

More information about this series at http://www.springer.com/series/7899

Maria Jose Escalona · Andres Jimenez Ramirez ·
Hugo Plácido Silva · Larry Constantine ·
Markus Helfert · Andreas Holzinger (Eds.)

Computer-Human Interaction Research and Applications

Second International Conference, CHIRA 2018
Seville, Spain, September 19–21, 2018
and Third International Conference, CHIRA 2019
Vienna, Austria, September 20–21, 2019
Revised Selected Papers

 Springer

Editors

Maria Jose Escalona
ETS Ingeniería Informática
Universidad de Sevilla
Sevilla, Spain

Hugo Plácido Silva
Instituto Superior Técnico
IT- Institute of Telecommunications
Lisbon, Portugal

Markus Helfert
Dublin City University
Dublin, Ireland

Andres Jimenez Ramirez
Escuela Técnica Superior de Ingeniería
Informática
Universidad de Sevilla
Sevilla, Spain

Larry Constantine
Madeira Interactive Technologies Institute
Funchal, Madeira, Portugal

Andreas Holzinger
Medical University of Graz
Graz, Austria

ISSN 1865-0929   ISSN 1865-0937 (electronic)
Communications in Computer and Information Science
ISBN 978-3-030-67107-5   ISBN 978-3-030-67108-2 (eBook)
https://doi.org/10.1007/978-3-030-67108-2

This Springer imprint is published by the registered company Springer Nature Switzerland AG
The registered company address is: Gewerbestrasse 11, 6330 Cham, Switzerland

Preface

This book includes extended and revised versions of a set of selected papers from the International Conference on Computer-Human Interaction Research and Applications, CHIRA 2018 and 2019 editions. The 2nd edition of CHIRA was held in Seville, Spain, in the period of September 19–21, 2018, and the 3rd edition was held in Vienna, Austria, in the period of September 20–21, 2019.

The purpose of the International Conference on Computer-Human Interaction Research and Applications (CHIRA) is to bring together professionals, academics and students who are interested in the advancement of research and practical applications of interaction design and human-computer interaction. Five parallel tracks were held, covering different aspects of Computer-Human Interaction, including Interaction Design, Human Factors, Entertainment, Cognition, Perception, User-Friendly Software and Systems, Pervasive Technologies and Interactive Devices.

CHIRA 2018 received 28 paper submissions from 19 countries, of which 14% were included in this book. CHIRA 2019 received 36 paper submissions from 23 countries, of which 8% were included in this book.

The papers were selected by the event chairs and their selection is based on a series of criteria including the classifications and comments provided by the program committee members, the session chairs' assessment and the program chairs' global view of all papers included in the technical program. The authors of selected papers were then invited to submit a revised and extended version of their papers having at least 30% innovative material.

The papers selected to be included in this book contribute to the understanding of relevant trends of current research on Computer-Human Interaction, including: Agent design for shape-shifting technology; User experience characterization based on Brain-Computer Interface (BCI) metrics; Auditory distractions taxonomization; Empowering citizen-environment Interaction; Impact on engagement with social object labels; HCI in music composition; and Assistive technologies design.

We would like to thank all the authors for their contributions and also the reviewers who have helped to ensure the quality of this publication. Moreover, we would like to thank the work of the CHIRA secretariat, who always supported the processes to achieve the highest possible quality.

September 2019

Maria Jose Escalona
Andres Jimenez Ramirez
Hugo Plácido Silva
Larry Constantine
Markus Helfert
Andreas Holzinger

Organization

Conference Co-chairs

2018

Markus Helfert — Maynooth University, Ireland

2019

Andreas Holzinger — Medical University of Graz, Austria
Markus Helfert — Maynooth University, Ireland
Larry Constantine — Madeira Interactive Technologies Institute, Portugal

Program Co-chairs

2018

Hugo Plácido Silva — IT- Instituto de Telecomunicações, Portugal
Larry Constantine — Madeira Interactive Technologies Institute, Portugal
Maria Jose Escalona — University of Seville, Spain
Andres Jimenez Ramirez — University of Seville, Spain

2019

Hugo Plácido Silva — IT- Instituto de Telecomunicações, Portugal
Andres Jimenez Ramirez — University of Seville, Spain

Program Committee

Served in 2018

David Ahlström — Alpen-Adria-Universität Klagenfurt, Austria
Bongsug Chae — Kansas State University, USA
Larry Constantine — Madeira Interactive Technologies Institute, Portugal
Sanda Erdelez — University of Missouri, USA
Jesus Favela — CICESE, Mexico
Peter Forbrig — University of Rostock, Germany
Kiel Gilleade — National Center for Supercomputing Applications, USA
Toni Granollers — University of Lleida, Spain
Bruno Heberlin — EPFL, Switzerland
Sylwia Hyniewska — World Hearing Centre, Poland
Andres Jimenez Ramirez — University of Seville, Spain
Maria Jose Escalona — University of Seville, Spain
Simeon Keates — University of Greenwich, UK

Carla Freitas	Universidade Federal do Rio Grande do Sul, Brazil
Diego Gachet	European University of Madrid, Spain
Karin Harbusch	Universität Koblenz-Landau, Germany
Beat Hirsbrunner	University of Fribourg, Switzerland
Martin Hitz	Alpen-Adria-Universität Klagenfurt, Austria
Victor Kaptelinin	Umeå University, Sweden
Adi Katz	SCE - Shamoon College of Engineering, Israel
Suzanne Kieffer	Université catholique de Louvain, Belgium
Gerard Kim	Korea University, Korea, Republic of
Gerhard Leitner	Alpen-Adria-Universität Klagenfurt, Austria
Lorenzo Magnani	University of Pavia, Italy
Federico Manuri	Politecnico di Torino, Italy
Frédéric Merienne	Arts et Métiers ParisTech, France
Daniel Mestre	Aix-Marseille University/CNRS, France
Max Mulder	TU Delft, Netherlands
Jaime Muñoz-Arteaga	Universidad Autónoma de Aguascalientes (UAA), Mexico
Radoslaw Niewiadomski	University of Genoa, Italy
Claudio Pinhanez	IBM Research, Brazil
Laura Ripamonti	Università degli Studi di Milano, Italy
Paul Rosenthal	University of Rostock, Germany
Andrea Sanna	Politecnico di Torino, Italy
Jean Vanderdonckt	Université catholique de Louvain, Belgium
Spyros Vosinakis	University of the Aegean, Greece
Marcus Winter	University of Brighton, UK

Invited Speakers

2018

Julio Abascal	University of the Basque Country/Euskal Herriko Unibertsitatea, Spain
Norbert Streitz	Founder and Scientific Director, Smart Future Initiative, Germany
Georgios N. Yannakakis	University of Malta, Malta
Eduardo Rocon	Consejo Superior de Investigaciones Científicas, Spain

2019

Kristina Höök	KTH Royal Institute of Technology, Sweden
Pietro Cipresso	Catholic University of the Sacred Heart, Italy
Helmut Windl	Panasonic Automotive Systems Europe GmbH, Germany

Contents

Display Placement and Design: Impact on Engagement with Social Object Labels in a Gallery Environment

Marcus Winter(✉) ⓘD

School of Computing, Engineering and Mathematics, University of Brighton, Brighton, UK
marcus.winter@brighton.ac.uk

Abstract. Considering placement and content design as key factors determining attention and engagement with interactive public displays, this paper reports on an empirical study investigating attention and engagement with social object labels as a particular instance of that display class in a museum context. It describes a field trial in a live gallery environment evaluating a range of display placements and designs. The study suggests that (i) placement has a major impact on attention and engagement; (ii) the attention potential of display placements can be quantified to predict attention and engagement rates; (iii) interaction- and information design only have a minor impact on some engagement metrics. The findings help to better understand how placement and design influence attention and engagement with public displays and underline the need for further research exploring these aspects in other contexts.

Keywords: HCI · Attention · Engagement · Interaction · Public displays · Pervasive displays · Social object labels · Interpretation · Participation · Museum

1 Introduction

Interactive public displays have been researched extensively over the past two decades, having their own series of international symposia since 2012 [22]. One of their many promising application areas is visitor engagement in museums. Besides providing guidance in concourse areas and curated information in galleries, interactive public displays also support participation, with display content created by visitors themselves rather than the institution. Social interpretation, where visitors share their own thoughts about exhibits and exhibition themes, is a particularly interesting application in this context, promising to contextualize and democratize museum interpretation [36, 48], enrich exhibitions and make them more inclusive [31], and support museums' higher-level educational goals by facilitating their transition from transfer learning to social-constructivist learning approaches [14, 19]. One research effort aiming to support social interpretation in museums are *social object labels* (SOLs) [51, 52], small interactive e-ink displays enabling visitors to add their own thoughts and interpretations to exhibits (Fig. 1). They give visitors a voice and a platform to relate exhibition themes to their own personal

© Springer Nature Switzerland AG 2021
M. J. Escalona et al. (Eds.): CHIRA 2018/CHIRA 2019, CCIS 1351, pp. 1–24, 2021.
https://doi.org/10.1007/978-3-030-67108-2_1

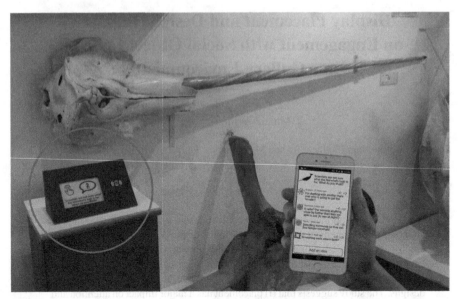

Fig. 1. SOL (circled) and related mobile application at the Booth Museum in Brighton, asking visitors to contribute their ideas on why narwhals have their particular tusk.

experiences and complement the museum's official interpretation on traditional object labels with socially constructed interpretations on SOLs.

As curated spaces with an educational agenda and their own rules and social norms, museums are complex environments with specific requirements and constraints for technology deployed in the gallery space. Of particular concern in this context is to carefully manage an economy of attention [45] by ensuring that technology is used "in ways that do not distract from the exhibition themes" [30:601] and "preserve the primacy of the object and aesthetic encounter" [46:3]. A critical design tension for SOLs is therefore to be inconspicuous enough to not divert visitors' attention from exhibits while being conspicuous enough to be noticed and to encourage engagement.

With placement and design identified as key factors in the HCI literature discussing attention and engagement with public displays, this paper reports on a field study assessing the impact of these two aspects on visitors' attention and engagement with SOLs in a live gallery environment. Its key contributions are to provide empirical evidence showing with high ecological validity that (i) display placement has a significant impact on attention and engagement; (ii) the *attention potential* of placements can be quantified to predict attention and engagement rates; (iii) variations in the interaction- and information design of SOLs only had a minor influence on some engagement metrics. The findings underline the need to better understand how placement-related factors impact on attention and engagement and advance the development of methods to quantify the attention potential of placements, which can help to inform the design, deployment and evaluation of interactive public displays.

The following sections review related work on attention and engagement with public displays, describe a field trial of SOLs at Science Gallery Dublin and discuss its findings with regard to the impact of display placement and design on visitors' attention and engagement. The paper concludes by discussing limitations of the study and sketching out future work towards a better understanding of effective placement and design of interactive public displays.

2　Related Work

Attention as "the process that brings a stimulus into consciousness" [25:25] is typically seen as a pre-condition for engagement, described as both the act of making initial contact and the state of being occupied with the object of attention [35]. The terms are widely discussed in the HCI literature, in particular in ubiquitous computing contexts where attention is often fragmented as multiple activities and stimuli vie for users' finite cognitive resources.

With regard to SOLs and their particular design tensions in museum environments, two of the most relevant research areas are ambient displays and interactive public displays. While the former is strongly influenced by the vision of *calm computing* [50] and seeks to minimize users' cognitive load of taking in information by blending into the environment and targeting their peripheral attention [27, 28], the latter is not constrained by such concerns. Important questions in public display research are simply how to attract the attention of audiences and, for interactive displays, how to communicate interactivity and encourage engagement.

In addition to these HCI perspectives, the field of museum studies offers highly relevant insights into attention and engagement in gallery environments. Besides providing detailed guidelines on label design, which can inform the information design of SOLs, this field also offers deep insights how visitors experience museums and how their attention and engagement is influenced by a wide range of factors.

2.1　Attention and Ambient Displays

Research into ambient information systems offers various models to conceptualize and structure attention into different states or realms. These include among others peripheral and focused attention [29]; primary, secondary and tertiary realms of attention [18]; pre-attention, in-attention, divided attention and focused attention [27]. Common to all these notions is that attention can be voluntary or involuntary [25], and that displays should address multiple forms of attention and support transitions between them. The latter typically involves targeting peripheral attention by default and escalating to focused attention and interaction when an exception occurs.

2.2　Attention and Engagement Models for Public Displays

Engagement models for public displays can be broadly classified into ad-hoc models, describing how displays react to users, and observational models, describing how users engage with displays [32]. Ad-hoc models typically employ proxemic interaction concepts [16, 47] to support specific stages in observational engagement models such as attracting attention and communicating interactivity.

Perhaps the best known observational model of engagement with interactive public displays is the audience funnel [32], which identifies six stages including passing by; viewing and reacting; subtle interaction; direct interaction; multiple interaction; and follow-up action. An earlier observational model [9] describes three levels of engagement, including peripheral awareness; focal awareness; and direct interaction. That work also discusses how displays can encourage users to transition between stages and increase their engagement. A model focusing in particular on engagement with public display games [15] defines seven interaction states including enter; glance; decode; observe; input; feedback; and result. The authors also discuss relevant design aspects to support users in each of these states. Finally, a model for engagement with public access systems [23] identifies four stages including attraction; learning; engagement; and disengagement. Guidelines how displays can support users in each of these stages are discussed in [24].

The majority of recommendations around attention and engagement with public displays relate to design aspects such as content type and representation [3, 8, 44], information design [3, 26, 44], calls to action [24], and learnability and usability [24, 26, 34]. However, some recommendations refer to placement aspects such as the height at which displays are installed [11, 20], the available space around them for interaction to take place [9, 24], the direction of people's movement within a space [20], the vicinity of other eye-catching objects [20] and, for multi-display settings, their spatial configuration [43]. All of these recommendations are helpful, however, there seems little discussion of their importance relative to each other or any interplay between them.

2.3 Attention and Engagement in Museums

Outside the HCI literature, the field of museum studies has a considerable body of work on attention and engagement in museums [e.g. 4–7, 39–41], which includes detailed guidelines on both the design and placement of interpretive resources to support visitors' engagement and learning. While these guidelines typically refer to static print labels and tangible information displays, some explicitly refer to "all type of media [including] print, audio and graphics" and presentation formats including "interactivity, sound, graphics, video, computers" [40:1].

Some placement-related heuristics in this domain have clear equivalents in public display research. For instance, the recommendation to place labels "within line of sight so that visitors do not have to turn, look up high, or down low" [4:120] can be related to the heuristic that public displays installed at eye-height and in the direction of people's movement receive more attention [20:241]. Others demonstrate a more holistic perspective that takes into account people's overall visiting experience. Examples of the latter are the consideration of satiation and fatigue when visitors progress through a exhibition as critical factors affecting their attention and engagement [6, 7].

2.4 Summary

The HCI literature on ambient displays and interactive public displays, as well as domain-specific literature on attention and engagement with interpretive resources in the context of museum studies, offer useful models and heuristics that can inform both the design and placement of interactive displays such as SOLs. However, they typically focus on single characteristic rather than taking into account multiple characteristics and their interplay, and they give no indication as to the relative importance of design- and placement-related factors. To address these aspects, we developed a method to quantify the attention potential of display placements based on multiple criteria, described in detail in [55], and in the present paper investigate how placement and design influence the levels of attention and engagement SOLs attract.

3 Social Object Labels

SOLs are an in-gallery commenting system designed to support visitor interpretation directly at the exhibit, when the experience is most immediate and most likely to prompt a response. The system consists of small (*inch-scale* [49]) interactive e-ink displays mounted next to exhibits, a related mobile application for visitors to add, browse, rate and flag comments, and an admin dashboard for museum staff to configure SOL displays, monitor their status and content, and moderate content flagged by visitors.

SOL designs evolved over several iterations, informed by research into visitors' perspectives on commenting in museums [53], museum professionals' requirements for in-gallery commenting platforms [54], a previous field trial at Science Gallery Dublin [56], as well as a theoretical design space analysis, technical prototyping, lab-based user testing and co-design sessions with users [52]. While a first evaluation [56] involved a version of SOLs limited to mobile interaction and a single design for all exhibits, the present field trial involves a version supporting both mobile and direct interaction on the SOL touch screen and a range of design variations that can be customized for specific exhibits.

Two models of direct interaction on the SOL touch screen were evaluated, one where the idle screen directly transitions to a help screen when touched (Fig. 2a) and one where the idle screen transitions to a browse screen when touched, enabling visitors to browse submitted comments, which then transitions to a help screen when visitors touch the call to action or the connection information on the browse screen (Fig. 2b). Both browse and help screens automatically revert to the idle screen when no interaction occurs for a certain time. In addition to touch screen interaction, SOLs also support mobile interaction, where visitors can browse, add, rate and flag comments (Fig. 2c).

4 Methodology

In order to evaluate SOLs in a realistic gallery environment, a field trial was carried out at Science Gallery Dublin, involving the deployment of four SOL displays in an exhibition called *Home\Sick* [38] for a duration of two weeks. As the field trial was part of a wider research effort exploring the design space for SOLs in museums, it was designed

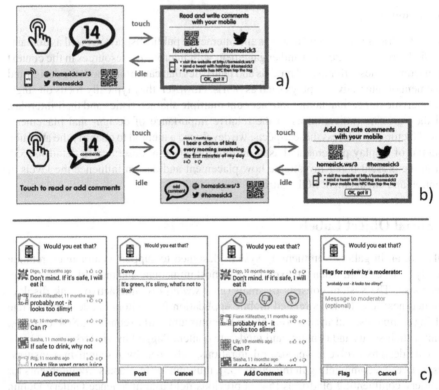

Fig. 2. SOL interaction models including direct touch screen interaction (a) without content browsing and (b) with content browsing, and (c) mobile interaction to browse, add, rate and flag comments after connecting a mobile device via QR code, NFC or URL.

to evaluate a range of aspects relating to visitors' attention, engagement, interaction and mental models of SOLs, as well as their attitudes to technology use and visitor interpretation in museums. This paper focuses in particular on how display placement and design impact on visitors' attention and engagement with SOLs. Research questions include:

1. To what extent does display placement affect attention and engagement with SOLs? We hypothesize that placement is a critical factor in how much attention and engagement SOLs attract.
2. Can the impact of placement on attention and engagement with SOLs be predicted? We hypothesize that individual ratings for placement-related factors known to impact attention and engagement can be combined to quantify the overall attention potential of placements, which in turn can be used to predict attention and engagement with SOLs.
3. To what extent does the information and interaction design affect attention and engagement with SOLs? We hypothesize that support for direct interaction increases overall engagement and that designs supporting content browsing on the SOL touch

screen, posing a questions to prompt and guide responses, or showing an image that relates the SOL to the exhibit and traditional object label, attract more attention and engagement than alternatives without these features.

The following sections discuss the deployment of SOLs in the gallery, describe the evaluated designs and data collection, and present the findings of the field trial with respect to these questions.

4.1 Placement in the Gallery

Four SOLs were installed in the gallery space, with the selection of exhibits guided by the idea of *social objects*, which provoke a reaction from visitors and stimulate debate [13, 42]. Besides common considerations for interactive public displays, such as having a sustained flow of people and sufficient space for interaction around them [24] and installing them at a suitable height [17], the placement of SOLs was also influenced by available mounting options, fit with the local ensemble, agreement of artists for SOLs to be installed at their exhibit and conformance with health and safety regulations. Figure 3 shows the four SOL installations in the order in which visitors would typically encounter them when making their way through the exhibition:

Fig. 3. SOLs (circled red) installed at four exhibits in the Home\Sick exhibition at Science Gallery Dublin. (Images used with permission, originally published in [55]).

- SOL No.1 was integrated with an exhibit called *Parasite Farm*, which explores how agricultural practices can become part of urban living. The SOL was placed on an empty shelf in a book case holding plant boxes, occupying a central position and affording convenient access for direct interaction (Fig. 3a).
- SOL No.2 was installed next to an exhibit called *LillyBot 2.0*, a personal microalgae farm that produces oxygen and Chlorella algae while binding carbon dioxide in the air. The SOL was placed to the right of the installation, requiring visitors to slightly bend down for direct interaction (Fig. 3b).
- SOL No.3 was integrated with an exhibit called *Ritual Machines*, which explores how technology can help to connect with family members away from home for extended periods. The SOL was placed next to a flip-dot matrix that can be controlled by visitors via two connected iPod touch devices, slightly set back but within easy reach of visitors operating the iPod on the left of the exhibit (Fig. 3c).
- SOL No.4 was installed next to an exhibit called *Dust Matter(s)*, which conceptualizes domestic dust in the home as an indicator of the occupants' outdoor activities. The SOL was placed in a prominent position below a large video screen within easy reach for direct interaction (Fig. 3d).

In order to better understand how placement might affect attention and engagement with SOLs, a method described in [55] was used to quantify the *attention potential* of placement options. The method uses a subset of factors known to affect the level of attention exhibits and interpretation materials receive during a museum visit [6, 7] and provides a simple rating scale to quantify them for specific placements.

All four factors relate to placement either in a local (exhibit) or global (gallery) context:

- Distraction: how many other stimuli are close by
- Competition: how much competition there is from other interaction opportunities
- Satiation: how often visitors have encountered a SOL in the gallery before
- Fatigue: at what stage during a visit they encounter the SOL

SOL installations were rated along each of these criteria before individual scores were combined to quantify the attention potential of each placement (Table 1).

4.2 Evaluated Designs

Evaluated design variations for the idle screen visitors encounter by default include versions with or without content browsing on the SOL touch screen, with or without a topical question to prompt visitor contributions, and with or without an image linking the SOL to the exhibit and traditional object label (Fig. 4).

The field trial deliberately includes designs that vary in more than one parameter (e.g. designs with both image and question) and designs that implement features differently (e.g. designs with and without content browsing display the question in different ways). By exploring design variations in different combinations, the study embraces the multi-variant character of the naturalistic environment, where many of the contextual factors influencing visitors' attention and engagement with SOLs are beyond the researcher's

Table 1. Quantified attention potential of display placements based on individual ratings on a scale of 1 (low) to 4 (high) for aspects known to affect attention and engagement in museums.

	Parasite Farm	LillyBot 2.0	Ritual Machines	Dust Matter(s)
Distraction	Little distraction apart from pot-plant above.	Sensor-driven exhibit dominates the scene.	Flip-dot display is extremely eye-catching.	Large video screen dominates the scene.
	[**1**] 2 3 4	1 2 [**3**] 4	1 2 3 [**4**]	1 2 [**3**] 4
Competition	Little spatula to dig in plant box on shelf below.	Control a blender by voice at exhibit close by.	Two iPods to control the flip-dot display.	No interaction possibilities close to the exhibit.
	1 [**2**] 3 4	1 2 [**3**] 4	1 2 3 [**4**]	[**1**] 2 3 4
Satiation	First SOL encountered in a typical visit.	Second SOL encountered in a typical visit.	Third SOL encountered in a typical visit.	Fourth SOL encountered in a typical visit.
	[**1**] 2 3 4	1 [**2**] 3 4	1 2 [**3**] 4	1 2 3 [**4**]
Fatigue	Third exhibit encountered in a typical visit.	Fourth exhibit encountered in a typical visit.	Sixth exhibit encountered in a typical visit.	Tenth exhibit encountered in a typical visit.
	[**1**] 2 3 4	1 [**2**] 3 4	1 2 [**3**] 4	1 2 3 [**4**]
Attention potential	$\dfrac{16 - 5}{16 - 4} = 92\%$	$\dfrac{16 - 10}{16 - 4} = 50\%$	$\dfrac{16 - 14}{16 - 4} = 17\%$	$\dfrac{16 - 12}{16 - 4} = 33\%$

control, and looks for findings that can be generalized beyond specific implementations and configurations.

In order for each design to have the same exposure with respect to exhibit, time of day and day of week, the installed SOLs automatically switched between designs following a fixed schedule. Layout switches took place at the midpoint of the daily gallery opening times for each day, resulting in two designs being active each day. Switches were synchronized to ensure that all SOLs in the gallery used the same design at any given time to leverage recognition and prior learning when visitors encounter them at different exhibits.

4.3 Data Collection and Analysis

Four data sets were used to assess attention and engagement with SOLs in the gallery. They include observations in the gallery, analytics data generated by SOL displays and the related mobile application, comments submitted to SOLs and in-house visitor numbers during the evaluation period collected via automatic visitor counters installed at Science Gallery Dublin.

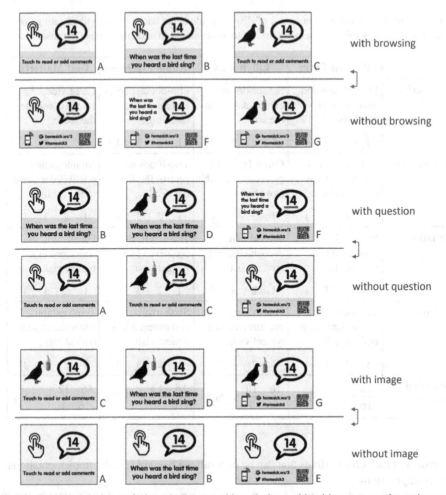

Fig. 4. Evaluated design variations A-G grouped into designs with/without content browsing on the SOL touch screen, with/without a question and with/without an exhibit-specific image.

Observations in the Gallery. Observations were carried out without explicit consent by visitors in order not to disturb their natural behavior and focused specifically on attention and engagement with SOLs. The researcher's conduct during observation sessions was informed by the British Psychological Society's code of ethics, which restricts observations "… to those situations in which persons being studied would reasonably expect to be observed by strangers, with reference to local cultural values and to the privacy of persons who, even while in a public space, may believe they are unobserved." [10:13].

Observation notes were recorded in a coding template and then transferred into a spreadsheet for analysis. Quantitative data was summarized, segmented and analyzed using standard statistical methods for user research discussed in [37]. Qualitative obser-vations were analyzed using a two-step emergent coding scheme described in [33] and then quantified where required.

Observations were carried out over six days with a combined observation time of 28 h and 56 min, during which a total of 812 encounters were observed. Encounters are conceptualized as situations where visitors have a clear chance to notice and engage with a SOL. As a minimum, this involves a visitor stopping at an exhibit. Visitors might then look at the exhibit, read the object label, look at and engage with the SOL in various ways.

The recorded observations are not evenly distributed among exhibits, SOL designs and SOL states. The data was therefore segmented and analyzed for each exhibit and design variation, with attention and engagement rates expressed as percentage values of observed encounters for each condition.

Analytics Data. Analytics data recording visitors' interaction with SOLs and the related mobile interaction was collected via an online API and related instrumentation of the client software. For direct interaction on the SOL touchscreen, interaction logs are struc-tured into sessions. A session starts with a visitor touching the SOL idle screen, last as long as there is touch interaction on the browse or help screens and end when displays time out and return to the idle screen. For mobile interactions, logs are generated for individual events, which can then be grouped into sessions via an anonymous but unique device ID. Mobile interaction sessions start with visitors connecting their device to a SOL and last as long as they browse, add, edit, rate or flag comments.

A total of 2,421 interaction logs were collected during the evaluation period. The data was prepared for analysis by excluding direct interaction logs involving admin tasks (e.g. display configuration, initial screen activation) and mobile interaction logs from demonstrations (e.g. to show how NFC works). The latter were identified through device IDs relating to the researcher and gallery staff. The resulting set of 1,921 visitor interaction logs used to analyze engagement and interaction with SOLs include 1,612 direct interaction logs and 309 mobile interaction logs.

A key difference between mobile and direct interaction logs is that the former relate to specific users, identified by their device, while the latter are anonymous and can involve multiple visitors, e.g. when one visitor abandons the SOL and another engages before the screen times out. In order to approximate the number of visitors engaging via the SOL touch screen, it is therefore necessary to determine the number of *user*

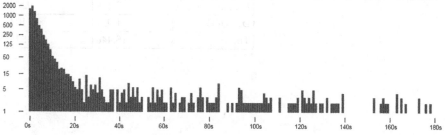

Fig. 5. Histogram of time intervals between interactions on SOL touch screen (logarithmic scale).

journeys in direct interaction session logs. For this purpose, a disengagement threshold was identified as the minimum time of inactivity after which it can be assumed that following interactions belong to a different user. This involved first classifying timing data into whole-second bins to analyze the distribution of time intervals between interactions (Fig. 5), and then using Jenks' natural breaks classification [21] to segment the time intervals into two clusters, representing touches during and between user journeys. The break point between these two clusters (55 s for designs with content browsing, 37 s for designs without content browsing) represents the disengagement threshold, which was used to determine the number of individual user journeys from direct interaction logs. Mobile interaction user journeys were determined simply by grouping mobile interaction logs by device ID and time. Total numbers based on 1,612 direct interaction logs and 309 mobile interaction logs include 2,031 direct interaction user journeys and 109 mobile interaction user journeys.

Submitted Comments. Visitor comments submitted to SOLs refer to a specific exhibit (placement) and can be attributed to specific designs via their time of submission and related analytics data. While contribution rates are an obvious measure of engagement, the small number of contributions during the evaluation period (n = 21, excluding seed comments) limits the reliability of any results based on this data set. It is included here nonetheless as it can give an indication of possible trends.

SGD Visitor Numbers. In order to establish a baseline of possible encounters with individual SOLs and design variations during the evaluation period, Science Gallery Dublin's in-house visitor numbers were consulted. The visitor numbers are based on automatic counters installed in the gallery and break down visits per day and time of day.

Table 2. Estimates of possible encounters with SOLs.

Possible encounters per placement		Possible encounters per design		
	All screens		All screens	Idle screen
Parasite Farm	2,822	Design A	2,602	1938
LillyBot 2.0	4,208	Design B	2,065	1538
Ritual Machines	4,208	Design C	2,223	1656
Dust Matter(s)	4,208	Design D	2,582	1923
Total	**15,446**	Design E	1,878	1667
		Design F	2,169	1925
		Design G	1,927	1710
		Total	**15,446**	**12,357**

Estimates of possible encounters per SOL and design are shown in Table 2. They take into account total visitor numbers for the evaluation period (4,208), daily visitor numbers, typical daily distribution of visitors over time, scheduled display times for specific SOL designs, down-times for SOL1 (Parasite Farm) due to a flat battery and the ratio between idle screen encounters and browse or help screen encounters from interaction logs. The estimates for possible encounters were used as a baseline to calculate engagement rates for SOL placements and designs from analytics data, allowing for triangulation with engagement rates from observations, which are based on actual rather than possible encounters.

5 Findings

5.1 Attention and Engagement Per Exhibit (Placement)

The data shows marked differences in attention and engagement rates between exhibits, despite all SOLs using the same design at any given time. Attention and engagement per exhibit (and by extension per SOL placement) follow a similar pattern, suggesting that they are influenced by similar factors:

- Observed attention to SOLs (Fig. 6a) is highest at Parasite Farm (86.6%), decreases at Lillybot 2.0 (60.8%), reaches its lowest point at Ritual Machines (47.0%) and picks up again for Dust Matter(s) (61.7%).
- Observed direct engagement with SOLs (Fig. 6b) is highest at Parasite Farm (31.4%), decreases at Lillybot 2.0 (10.5%), reaches its lowest point at Ritual Machines (4.3%) and picks up again for Dust Matter(s) (10.9%).
- Direct engagement with SOLs from analytics data (Fig. 6c) is highest at Parasite Farm (23.7%), decreases at Lillybot 2.0 (10.0%), reaches its lowest point at Ritual Machines (5.4%) and picks up again for Dust Matter(s) (7.9%).
- Mobile engagement with SOLs from analytics data (Fig. 6d) is highest at Parasite Farm (1.28%), decreases at LillyBot 2.0 (0.97%), reaches its lowest point at Ritual Machines (0.38%) and stays at this level for Dust Matter(s).
- The contribution rate for SOLs (Fig. 6e) is highest at Parasite Farm (0.25%), decreases at LillyBot 2.0 (0.17%), reaches its lowest point at Ritual Machines (0.05%) and increases again for Dust Matter(s) (0.12%).
- For reference, Fig. 6f shows the quantified attention potential for each SOL placement as discussed above, which is highest at Parasite Farm (92%), decreases at LillyBot 2.0 (50%), reaches its lowest point at Ritual Machines (17%) and increases again for Dust Matter(s) (33%).

The data reflects visitors' qualified progression from attention to engagement to contribution, with large numbers failing to progress at each stage. Regardless of absolute numbers, the different data sets reveal a consistent pattern, suggesting they are influenced by similar factors. There are strong and significant correlations between observed attention and observed direct engagement ($r = 0.99$, $t = 8.69$, $p < 0.01$), engagement rates from analytics data ($r = 0.97$, $t = 5.52$, $p < 0.01$) and contribution rates ($r = 0.96$, $t = 4.56$, $p < 0.01$). The only data set not strongly and significantly correlating to

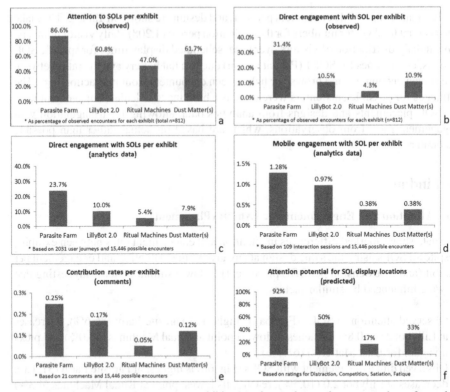

Fig. 6. Attention and engagement per exhibit: (a) observed attention, as number of people observed to look at SOL divided by number of encounters for that exhibit; (b) observed engagement, as number of people observed to engage with SOL divided by number of encounters for that exhibit; (c) engagement on SOL touch screen from analytics data, as number of user journeys on a SOL divided by number of potential encounters for that exhibit; (d) mobile engagement from analytics data, as number of mobile interaction sessions with a SOL divided by number of potential encounters for that exhibit; (e) contribution rates, as number of comments submitted to a SOL divided by number of potential encounters for that exhibit; and (f) the quantified attention potential for each SOL placement for reference.

observed attention is mobile engagement ($r = 0.83$, $t = 2.08$, $p = 0.08$), which remains flat between Ritual Machines and Dust Matter(s). While this might be attributed to the small number of people who engaged in mobile interaction, an alternative interpretation is that the additional physical and cognitive effort associated with connecting a mobile device to the display becomes more relevant in the later stages of a visit when museum fatigue [6, 7, 12] sets in.

5.2 Predicted vs Measured Attention and Engagement

Regarding the predictive power of the quantified attention potential for each SOL placement, the data shows strong and significant correlations (Table 3) not only between attention potential and observed attention rates but also between attention potential and observed direct engagement, direct engagement from analytics data, mobile engagement and contribution rates (Fig. 7). While these correlations do not imply causality, they suggests that placement-related factors are a good indicator of how much attention and engagement a display receives.

Table 3. Correlation between attention potential and measured attention and engagement. (Table used with permission, originally published in [55]).

	Attention potential	Attention (observed)	Direct Eng. (observed)	Direct Eng. (analytics)	Mobile Eng. (analytics)	Contrib. (comments)
Parasite Farm	91.7%	86.6%	31.4%	23.7%	1.28%	0.25%
LillyBot 2.0	50.0%	60.8%	10.5%	10.0%	0.97%	0.17%
Ritual Machines	16.7%	47.0%	4.3%	5.4%	0.38%	0.05%
Dust Matter(s)	33.3%	61.7%	10.9%	7.9%	0.38%	0.12%
Correlation r	-	0.972	0.967	0.978	0.936	0.982
t-value	-	5.802	5.387	6.675	3.755	7.315
p-value	-	0.0011	0.0017	0.0005	0.0094	0.0003

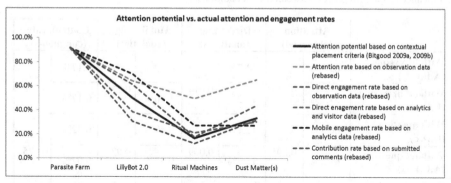

Fig. 7. Correlation between attention potential and measured attention and engagement. The diagram shows values proportionally rebased to the attention potential of Parasite Farm. (Diagram used with permission, originally published in [55]).

While the correlation is based on only four data points per series and the predicted attention potential on only four placement-related criteria, the results are promising and warrant future research into validating this method and adapting in for other environments. Potential benefits include using quantified attention potential as an additional vector to inform object selection and local display placement, as a baseline to scope expectations about attention and engagement with displays, and to inform mitigating design choices, e.g. using a more luminous display or a more conspicuous casing to compensate for the low attention potential of a placement.

5.3 Attention and Engagement Per Design

Reflecting the fact that design variations pertain primarily to the idle screen (Fig. 4) rather than browse or help screens, the measured attention and engagement rates per design are based on interaction sessions, which always start with the idle screen, rather than user journeys, which can equally start with browse or help screens encountered by visitors when a SOL was abandoned by a previous user and has not yet timed out and reverted to the idle screen. Accordingly, the baseline for engagement rates per design are potential encounters with SOL idle screens rather than potential encounters with SOLs in general (Table 2).

The results provide a mixed picture regarding visitors' attention and engagement with the evaluated SOL designs, not always supporting reliable conclusions about the effectiveness of related design parameters. Table 4 shows that in many cases the differences in attention and engagement rates between these designs did not reach a level of statistical significance. This applies in particular to observed attention, mobile engagement and contribution rates, the latter two mainly due to the small numbers involved. The following paragraphs focus on the four design variations where differences in engagement rates did reach a significant level:

Table 4. Attention, direct engagement, mobile engagement and contribution rates for SOL designs with or without browsing, with or without question and with or without image; p values indicate significance of the differences between these conditions.

	Attention (observed)		Direct Eng. (analytics)		Mobile Eng. (analytics)		Contrib. rate (comments)	
With browsing (A,B,C,D)	63.7%	p = 0.113	13.7%	p = 0.014	0.79%	p = 0.226	0.17%	p = 0.996
Without browsing (E,F,G)	57.7%		12.2%		1.00%		0.17%	
With question (B,D,F)	60.7%	p = 0.895	12.1%	p = 0.009	0.89%	p = 0.924	0.22%	p = 0.025
Without question (A,C,E,G)	61.2%		13.7%		0.88%		0.07%	
With image (C,D,G)	63.3%	p = 0.220	11.6%	p < 0.001	0.76%	p = 0.196	0.15%	p = 0.951
Without image (A,B,E,F)	58.6%		14.1%		0.98%		0.16%	

Figure 8b shows that direct engagement rates were higher for designs with browsing (13.7%) than for designs without browsing (12.2%). While the difference is small (1.5%), it is statistically significant (p = 0.014) and suggests that designs with browsing are overall a better choice in terms of encouraging visitor engagement. However, given that these engagement rates reflect engagement with the idle screen, it can be assumed that it is not the browsing functionality itself causing higher engagement rates but related differences in the idle screen design, which shows a question or call to action for designs with browsing, as opposed to information on how to connect a mobile phone for designs without browsing (Fig. 4). This assumption is supported by numbers including encounters with browse and help screens and using all possible encounters as baseline, which results in engagement rates of 11.8% for designs with browsing and 11.1% for designs without browsing, not reaching statistical significance (p = 0.153). The results suggest that a question or call to action is more effective in encouraging direct interaction on the SOL touch screen than information explaining how to connect a mobile phone to browse and add comments.

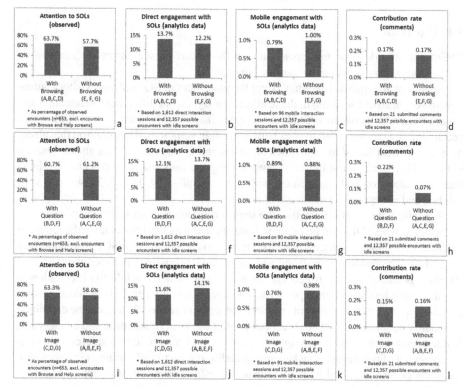

Fig. 8. Attention, direct engagement, mobile engagement and contribution rates for SOL designs (a–d) with or without browsing, (e–h) with or without question and (i–l) with or without image.

Figure 8f shows that direct engagement rates were lower for designs with a question (12.1%) than for designs without a question (13.7%). The difference of 1.6% is statistically significant (p = 0.009) and suggests that designs asking a question to prompt and focus visitor responses are less effective in encouraging visitor engagement on the SOL touch screen than designs showing a call to action.

Figure 8j shows that direct engagement rates were lower for designs with an image (11.6%) than for designs without an image (14.1%). The difference of 2.5% is statistically significant (p < 0.001) and suggests that designs showing an image linking the SOL to the exhibit are less effective in encouraging visitor engagement on the touch screen than designs showing a generic icon visually communicating support for touch screen interaction.

Figure 8h shows that contribution rates were higher for designs with a question (0.22%) than for designs without a question (0.07%). The difference of 0.15% is statistically significant (p = 0.025) and suggests that designs asking a question to prompt and focus visitor responses are more effective in encouraging visitors to submit a comment than designs showing a generic call to action. However, due to the overall low number of comments submitted during the evaluation period (n = 21) more data is required to confirm this interpretation.

5.4 Discussion

The results provide clear answers to some of the research questions in this study while not supporting any firm conclusions for others.

Regarding the question to what extent the placement of SOLs affects visitors' attention and engagement with them, the results show significant differences in attention and engagement rates between individual SOL installations, which far outweigh the small and at times insignificant differences between design variations. They confirm that placement is a critical factor in how much attention and engagement SOLs attract, and are in line with reports in the literature emphasizing the importance of placement-related factors on attention and engagement with public displays [9, 11, 20, 24, 43] and with exhibits and interpretation materials in museums [4–7].

Regarding the question whether the impact of placement on visitors' attention and engagement with SOLs can be predicted, we applied a method to quantify the attention potential of display placements described in [55] to each of the four SOL installations in the gallery. The results show strong and significant correlations between the predicted attention potential and measured attention and engagement. While the correlation is based on only four data points per series and does not imply causality, it seems to support the hypothesis that ratings of individual placement-related factors can be combined to quantify an attention potential that can predict the level of attention and engagement SOLs receive. If these predictive qualities can be confirmed in further studies, the attention potential of placements can become an additional vector informing object selection and local positioning, and help to evaluate the effectiveness of SOL deployments by providing a baseline for attention and engagement.

Regarding the question how information and interaction design affect attention and engagement with SOLs, the results provide qualified support for some hypotheses while rejecting others. The results show no significant differences in attention rates between design variations, however, they do show significant differences in direct engagement rates:

- The results confirm the hypothesis that designs supporting direct interaction attract more engagement than designs without content browsing. While the data does not support any conclusions about the effectiveness of interaction models per se in encouraging engagement, it clearly shows that designs displaying questions or calls to action on the idle screen have significantly higher direct engagement rates than designs displaying information how to connect a mobile device via a QR code, NFC and URL.

This is in line with earlier findings of some museum visitors having negative attitude towards QR codes, leading them to ignore interaction opportunities, and the need to de-emphasize technical aspects in the user interface [56].

- The results reject the hypothesis that designs posing a question to prompt visitors and focus their responses attract more engagement than designs showing a generic call to action. Instead, the data shows that designs with a generic call to action have significantly higher direct engagement rates than designs posing a question, even though some of the underlying reasoning for posing a question is vindicated by designs with a question having higher contribution rates than designs with a generic prompt. Together, these findings support claims in the literature that questions can encourage visitor interpretation by directing and scaffolding responses [42], however, they also show that generic calls to action are a more effective way to encourage engagement with SOLs in first place.

- The results reject the hypothesis that designs showing an image relating the SOL to the exhibit and object label attract more engagement than designs showing a generic touch screen icon. Instead, the data shows that designs with a generic touch screen icon have significantly higher direct engagement rates than designs showing an exhibit-specific image. While not denying that the image helped to integrate SOLs with the local information environment [8] of exhibits, it clearly shows that this does not necessarily translate to increased engagement.

Overall, the findings support some of our assumptions how placement and design affect attention and engagement with SOLs, while they qualify and reject others. Placement clearly has a strong impact on attention and various engagement measures, outweighing any effects of interaction and information design. The results also suggest that attention and engagement can be predicted, at least in a gallery context, by assessing the attention potential of placements using the method proposed in [55]. By comparison, the effects of design variations are less pronounced, only producing significant differences for some engagement measures while being inconclusive for others.

6   Limitations

In line with calls in the literature that ubiquitous computing technologies should be evaluated in realistic environments [1, 2, 18], the emphasis of this study was on ecological validity, as reflected in the live gallery deployment and non-obtrusive data collection. As a consequence, however, the research is subject to the museum's constraints, practices and natural visitor flow, limiting control over important parameters. In addition, the limited timeframe in which the study was carried out further constrained the research design. Limitations relating to one or more of these factors include:

- The study does not involve clear A/B testing as the evaluated designs vary in more than one parameter as well as their exact implementation. While this decreases internal validity, it increases external validity by exploring design variations in different combinations, making it more likely that findings can be generalized beyond specific configurations.

- The study involves a large number of observations, however, it can be difficult to reliably judge from observations whether someone looks at and actually notices a SOL, which introduces an error margin for observed attention rates.
- Engagement rates are based on user journeys and potential encounters, both of which are approximations. In order to avoid overstating engagement rates, minimum values for user journeys and maximum values for potential encounters were used.
- The low levels of mobile engagement and content contribution against the large number of potential encounters makes conventional thresholds for statistical significance problematic, reducing the validity of results relating to these data sets.
- The attention potential of SOL installations is based on a subset of placement-related factors identified in [6, 7] to affect visitors' attention in museums, but is likely to be influenced by many other factors. The strong and significant correlation with actual attention and engagement rates is based on only four installations and does not imply causality. More research is needed to integrate additional factors influencing attention potential and to assess the validity and utility of the method.

With regard to transferability, many findings of this evaluation are general enough to be applicable to other contexts and environments. While emerging from a study investigating attention and engagement with SOLs in particular, it is hoped that they are useful to researchers exploring other interactive public display concepts.

7 Conclusions

Drawing on heuristics and guidelines in the literature describing how placement- and design-related factors impact on people's attention and engagement with public displays on the one hand, and with interpretation resources in museums on the other hand, this paper reports findings from an empirical study evaluating the effects of placement and design in a field trial of SOLs at Science Gallery Dublin.

It confirms placement as a key factor in how much attention and engagement displays receive and suggests that attention and engagement rates can be predicted by quantifying the attention potential of placements. The proposed method to quantify the attention potential of placements [55] combines ratings along four aspects known to affect attention and engagement in a museum context, however, the principle of combining ratings for several factors to quantify an attention potential easily transfers to other contexts, warranting further research into adapting the method to incorporate other placement-related factors described in the literature and evaluating it with more deployments and in different environments.

Putting into perspective the importance of design-related heuristics discussed in the literature, the field trial found that variations in the interaction- and information-design of SOLs had no significant effect on attention rates and only minor effects reaching significance on some engagement metrics. Specifically, they indicate that designs showing a generic call to action, displaying a touch screen icon and not presenting technical information on the idle screen attract more direct engagement on the SOL touch screen than designs posing a question, displaying an exhibit-specific image or presenting technical information how to connect a mobile device. They also indicate that designs posing a questions attract more contributions, vindicating recommendations in the literature in this respect [42], but otherwise found no significant differences between designs for other engagement measures.

Despite the limitations discussed above, this paper makes important contributions by showing with high ecological validity that display placement has an overriding effect on attention and engagement, and that this effect can be predicted to some degree by quantifying the attention potential of display placements. This can help to scope expectations about attention and engagement for specific deployments and support public display evaluations by putting into context design-related factors that might impact on specific engagement metrics.

While the study involved SOLs as a specific instance of interactive displays, deployed in a gallery environment as a specific instance of a public use environment, many of is findings are general enough to be relevant to other display types and environments. They warrant future research developing more general methods to quantify the attention potential of display placements, advancing our understanding how placement and design influence attention and engagement, and helping towards increasing the effectiveness and impact of public display applications.

Acknowledgements. We would like to thank Science Gallery Dublin for sharing their valuable insights and supporting this research during the field trial. We also thank visitors to the Home\Sick exhibition for unwittingly supporting this research with their curiosity and engagement in the gallery space.

References

1. Abowd, G.: What next, ubicomp? Celebrating an intellectual disappearing act. In: Proceedings of 14th International Conference on Ubiquitous Computing, pp. 1–10. ACM (2012)
2. Abowd, G., Mynatt, E.: Charting past, present, and future research in ubiquitous computing. ACM Trans. Comput. Hum. Interact. 7(1), 29–58 (2000)
3. Ames, M., Dey, A.: Description of design dimensions and evaluation for Ambient Displays. Technical Report CSD-02-1211. EECS Department, University of California (2002). http://www.eecs.berkeley.edu/Pubs/TechRpts/2002/6193.html. Accessed 24 May 2020
4. Bitgood, S.: The ABCs of label design. Visitor Stud. Theory Res. Pract. 3(1), 115–129 (1991)
5. Bitgood, S.: The role of attention in designing effective interpretive labels. J. Interpret. Res. 5(2), 31–45 (2000)
6. Bitgood, S.: Museum fatigue: a critical review. Visitor Stud. 12(2), 93–111 (2009)
7. Bitgood, S.: When is "museum fatigue" not fatigue? Curator 52(2), 193–202 (2009)
8. Brewer, J.: Factors in designing effective ambient displays. In: Proceedings of 6th International Conference on Ubiquitous Computing, pp. 1–2. ACM (2004)
9. Brignull, H., Rogers, Y.: Enticing people to interact with large public displays in public spaces. In: Proceedings of 9th International Conference on Human-Computer Interaction, pp. 1–5. IOS Press (2003)
10. British Psychological Society: Code of Ethics and Conduct. BPS (2009). https://www.bps.org.uk/files/code-ethics-and-conduct-2009pdf. Accessed 24 May 2020
11. Cheverst, K., Fitton, D., Dix, A.: Exploring the evolution of office door displays. In: O'Hara, K., et al. (eds.) Public and Situated Displays: Social and Interactional Aspects of Shared Display Technologies, Ch. 6. Kluwer (2003)

12. Davey, G.: What is museum fatigue? Visitor Stud. Today **8**(3), 17–21 (2005)
13. Engeström, J.: Why some social network services work and others don't - or: the case for object-centered sociality. Blog post 13 April 2005. http://www.zengestrom.com/blog/2005/04/why-some-social-network-services-work-and-others-dont-or-the-case-for-object-centered-sociality.html. Accessed 24 May 2020
14. Falk, J.H., Dierking, L. D.: Learning from Museums. Visitor Experiences and the Making of Meaning. AltaMira Press, Walnut Creek (2000)
15. Finke, M., Tang, A., Leung, R., Blackstock, M.: Lessons learned: game design for large public displays. In: Proceedings of 3rd International Conference on Digital Interactive Media in Entertainment and Arts, pp. 10–12. ACM (2008)
16. Greenberg, S.: Opportunities for proxemic interactions in ubicomp (keynote). In: Campos, P., Graham, N., Jorge, J., Nunes, N., Palanque, P., Winckler, M. (eds.) INTERACT 2011. LNCS, vol. 6946, pp. 3–10. Springer, Heidelberg (2011). https://doi.org/10.1007/978-3-642-23774-4_3
17. Hardy, R., Rukzio, E., Holleis, P., Wagner, M.: Mobile interaction with static and dynamic NFC-based displays. In: Proceedings of 12th International Conference on Human Computer Interaction with Mobile Devices and Services, pp. 123–132. ACM (2010)
18. Hazlewood, W.R., Coyle, L.: On ambient information systems. Int. J. Ambient Comput. Intell. **1**(2), 1–12 (2009)
19. Hein, G.E.: The constructivist museum. J. Educ. Mus. **16**, 21–23 (1995)
20. Huang, Elaine M., Koster, A., Borchers, J.: Overcoming assumptions and uncovering practices: when does the public really look at public displays? In: Indulska, J., Patterson, Donald J., Rodden, T., Ott, M. (eds.) Pervasive 2008. LNCS, vol. 5013, pp. 228–243. Springer, Heidelberg (2008). https://doi.org/10.1007/978-3-540-79576-6_14
21. Jenks, G.F.: The data model concept in statistical mapping. In: International Yearbook of Cartography, vol. 7, pp. 186–190 (1967)
22. José, R., Huang, E. (eds.) In: Proceedings of Internationa Symposium on Pervasive Displays. ACM (2012)
23. Kearsley, G.: Public Access Systems: Bringing Computer Power to the People. Ablex Publishing Corporation (1994)
24. Kules, B., Kang, H., Plaisant, C., Rose, A.: Immediate usability: a case study of public access design for a community photo library. Interact. Comput. **16**(6), 1171–1193 (2004)
25. Mack, A., Rock, I.: Inattentional Blindness, vol. 33. MIT Press, Cambridge (1998)
26. Mankoff, J., Dey, A.: A Practical Guide To Designing Ambient Displays. In: Ohara, K., Churchill, E. (eds.) Public and Situated Displays, pp. 1–21. Kluwer (2003)
27. Matthews, T., Rattenbury, T., Carter, S., Dey, A., Mankoff, J.: A peripheral display toolkit. Technical Report No. UCB/CSD-03-1258. University of California (2003)
28. Matthews, T.L., Forlizzi, J., Rohrbach, S.: Designing Glanceable Peripheral Displays. Technical Report No. UCB/EECS-2006-113. University of California (2006)
29. Matthews, T., Rattenbury, T., Carter, S.: Defining, designing, and evaluating peripheral displays: an analysis using activity theory. Hum. Comput. Interact. **22**(1–2), 221–261 (2007)
30. Maye, L.A., McDermott, F.E., Ciolfi, L., Avram, G.: Interactive exhibitions design - what can we learn from cultural heritage professionals? In: Proceedings of 8th Nordic Conference on Human-Computer Interaction, pp. 598–607. ACM (2014)
31. McLean, K.: Museum exhibitions and the dynamics of dialogue. Daedalus **128**(3), 83–107 (1999)

32. Michelis, D., Müller, J.: The audience funnel: observations of gesture based interaction with multiple large displays in a city center. Int. J. Hum. Comput. Interact. 27(6), 562–579 (2011)
33. Miles, M.B., Huberman, A.M.: Qualitative Data Analysis. Sage, Newbury Park (1984)
34. Müller, J., Alt, F., Michelis, D., Schmidt, A.: Requirements and design space for interactive public displays. In: Proceedings of 18th International Conference on Multimedia, pp. 1285–1294. ACM (2010)
35. Peters, C., Castellano, G., de Freitas, S.: An exploration of user engagement in HCI. In: Proceedings of International Workshop on Affective-Aware Virtual Agents and Social Robots, pp. 1–3. ACM (2009)
36. Sandell, R.: Social inclusion, the museum and the dynamic of sectoral change. Mus. Soc. 1(1), 45–62 (2003)
37. Sauro, J., Lewis, J.R.: Quantifying the User Experience. Morgan Kaufmann, Burlington (2012)
38. Science Gallery Dublin: Home\Sick: Post-Domestic Bliss. Science Gallery Dublin (2015). https://dublinsciencegallery.com/homesick/. Accessed 24 May 2020
39. Screven, C.G.: The museum as a responsive learning environment. Mus. News 47(10), 7–10 (1969)
40. Screven, C.G.: Motivating visitors to read labels. ILVS Rev. 2(2), 183–211 (1992)
41. Serrell, B.: Exhibit Labels: An Interpretive Approach. Alta Mira Press (1996)
42. Simon, N.: The participatory museum. Museum 2.0 (2010). http://www.participatorymuseum.org/. Accessed 24 May 2020
43. Ten Koppel, M., Bailly, G., Müller, J., Walter, R.: Chained displays: configurations of public displays can be used to influence actor-, audience-, and passer-by behavior. In: Proceedings of SIGCHI Conference on Human Factors in Computing Systems, pp. 317–326. ACM (2012)
44. Tomittsch, M., Kappel, K., Lehner, A., Grechenig, T.: Towards a taxonomy for ambient information systems. In: Proceedings of 5th International Conference on Pervasive Computing, vol. 44. Springer (2007)
45. Tröndle, M., Wintzerith, S.: A museum for the twenty-first century: the influence of "sociality" on art reception in museum space. Mus. Manage. Curatorship 27(5), 461–486 (2012)
46. Vom Lehn, D., Heath, C.: Displacing the object: mobile technologies and interpretive resources. Arch. Mus. Inform. 2 (2003)
47. Wang, M., Boring, S., Greenberg, S.: Proxemic peddler: a public advertising display that captures and preserves the attention of a passerby. In: Proceedings of International Symposium on Pervasive Displays, pp. 1–6. ACM (2012)
48. Weil, S.E.: From being about something to being for somebody: the ongoing transformation of the american museum. Daedalus 128(3), 229–258 (1999)
49. Weiser, M.: The computer for the 21st century. Sci. Am. 3(3), 3–11 (1991)
50. Weiser, M., Seely Brown, J.: Designing calm technology. PowerGrid J. 1(01), 1–5 (1996)
51. Winter, M.: Social object labels: supporting social object annotation with small pervasive displays. In: Proceedings of International Conference on Pervasive Computing and Communications, pp. 489–494. IEEE (2014)
52. Winter, M.: A design space for social object labels in museums. Ph.D. thesis. School of Computing, Engineering and Mathematics, University of Brighton (2016)
53. Winter, M.: Visitor perspectives on commenting in museums. Mus. Manage. Curatorship 33(5), 484–505 (2018)
54. Winter, M.: Requirements for an in-gallery social interpretation platform: a museum perspective. In: Proceedings of 3rd International Conference on Computer-Human Interaction Research and Applications, pp. 66–77. INSTICC ScitePress (2019)

55. Winter, M., Brunswick, I., Williams, D.: Quantifying the attention potential of pervasive display placements. In: Proceedings of 2nd International Conference on Computer-Human Interaction Research and Applications, CHIRA, vol. 1, pp. 70–80 (2018). ISBN 978-989-758-328-5. ISSN 2184-3244. https://doi.org/10.5220/0007223800700080
56. Winter, M., Gorman, M.J., Brunswick, I., Browne, D., Williams, D., Kidney, F.: Fail better: lessons learned from a formative evaluation of social object labels. In: Proceedings of 8th International Workshop on Personalized Access to Cultural Heritage, pp. 1–9. CEUR Workshop Proceedings (2015)

Learning from Errors Designing Assistive Technology

Julio Abascal$^{(\boxtimes)}$ (iD)

Egokituz Laboratory of Human-Computer Interaction for Special Needs,
School of Informatics, University of the Basque Country/Euskal Herriko Unibertsitatea,
Manuel Lardizabal 1, 20018 Donostia, Spain
julio.abascal@ehu.eus

> *If you shut the door to all errors, truth will be
> shut out.*
>
> Rabindranath Tagore

Abstract. From its foundation in 1985, the Egokituz Laboratory of HCI for Special needs has researched the application of diverse HCI methodologies and technologies to enhance the inclusion and digital accessibility of people with diverse types of disabilities. Over this time we have discovered that the human side of the HCI requires specific attention that technology oriented people -that's us- are not always qualified to provide. In this talk, I will review some mistakes that I hope we have learned from. I will also present our approaches to overcoming these mistakes.

Keywords: Digital accessibility · Assistive technology · User centered design · Users' participation

1 Rationale

This paper elaborates on some ideas I presented in a keynote speech to the CHIRA/NEUROTECHNIX 2018 conferences held in Seville in December 2018.

In 1980, C.A.R. Hoare received the ACM Turing Award. A year later his award winning lecture was published [1] (I thing that this delightful paper should be recommended to every Software Engineering student). When I read it, I understood that some bad decisions and design failures could provide guidance for future success if they were adequately interpreted. In the introduction of that paper, Professor Hoare wrote: "Instead of repeating the abstruse technicalities of my trade, I would like to talk informally about myself, my personal experiences, my hopes and fears, my modest successes, and my rather less modest failures. [...] Besides, failures are much more fun to hear about afterwards; they are not so funny at the time".

© Springer Nature Switzerland AG 2021
M. J. Escalona et al. (Eds.): CHIRA 2018/CHIRA 2019, CCIS 1351, pp. 25–40, 2021.
https://doi.org/10.1007/978-3-030-67108-2_2

On a similar theme of mistakes and failures, Simeon Keates recently published a paper entitled "When universal access is not quite universal enough: case studies and lessons to be learned" [2] (I think that this remarkable paper should be recommended to every Digital Accessibility student). In this paper too, the leading idea is that failures, bad results and blunders can also be useful to avoid errors in future research.

Even if I cannot compare my experience with the ones presented by these prestigious professors, I think that I have collected a number of bad decisions (made both by me and by other people) that could be worth discussing and interpreting in order to obtain new knowledge. This is quite a risky approach for a regular lecture, but it should be acceptable for a less strict keynote speech[1]. I have considered it more prudent to avoid mentioning names or pictures of failed works.

2 *Egokituz* Laboratory of HCI for Special Needs

Let me start by introducing our laboratory. *Egokituz* (meaning "adapting" in the Basque Language), is the Laboratory of Human-Computer Interaction for Special Needs. We created it in 1985 for the application of computer technologies to enhance the digital accessibility and social inclusion of people with diverse types of disabilities.

All the three "founders" were "hardware people". Soon we discovered the need for HCI theories and tools, in order to design equipment and services well adapted to the actual users' needs. We were interested in diverse methodologies, such as User Centered Design, Cognitive Ergonomics, Participatory Design or Formal User Testing. However, at that time, we did not have many opportunities to study all of these matters. We were unable to take courses on Human-Computer Interaction, Assistive Technology, or Design with Users with Disabilities. Therefore, in addition to reading almost everything that came our way and attending every possible conference and workshop on these topics, we decided to collaborate with other people who had experience in this field.

Thanks to this strategy, by 1990 our laboratory had obtained some experience and reputation at a national level [3]. For this reason, we received invitations to participate in diverse international initiatives where, in addition to contributing with our experience, we absorbed a great deal of knowledge and experience from researchers in accessibility from around the world.

- In 1990, the European Commission invited us to join a team of 25 European experts that developed a European study, the TIDE[2] Market Survey (1990) with the intention of laying the foundations for a European accessibility research and development plan. This initial experience was followed by frequent participation in successive calls included in the FP 4 and in the subsequent European R&D Framework Programmes,

---

[1] After giving this talk, I had the pleasure of having dinner with Professor Larry Constantine. He had spent my entire presentation taking pictures of my slides with a huge telephoto lens, and at the end of the session he asked several questions, so I was a bit concerned about his opinion. At the dinner, he told me that the pictures were for his wife who was in the United States. "I hope she enjoys your talk as much as I did". Evidently, his friendly words relaxed me a lot.

[2] TIDE Programme: Technology for the Integration of Disabled and Elderly People.

in which we collaborated in playing diverse roles, such as expert, reviewer, evaluator or advisor.

- We were also invited to be part of the Management Committee of the COST 219 bis Telecommunications: Access for Disabled and Elderly People (1998-2001) and COST 219ter Accessibility of Services and Terminals for Next Generation Networks (2003-2006). Highly reputed European researchers with very diverse backgrounds participated in these actions, in which we also contributed and learned.
- In 1992, the Spanish Office for Science and Technology appointed me to represent Spain in the IFIP Technical Committee 13 on HCI, in which we funded the working group WG13.3 on HCI and Disability.

All these collaborations were significant for the future evolution of our laboratory. They opened our minds to novel methodologies well suited to our digital accessibility goals. However, I must confess that our main source of knowledge and experience came from real users with disabilities and their associations, families, and care workers.

From the beginning we developed -or collaborated with- several research projects in which we had achieved some success and suffered several failures. Making mistakes is unavoidable. The important thing is to detect them, analyze them and avoid them in the future. I would need a full session to analyze each case in detail. For the sake of brevity let me try to briefly summarize and comment on some unsuccessful approaches and trials

3   Three (Wrong) Reasons to Start an R&D Project on Accessibility

3.1   We Can Do It Better and Cheaper

In 1985, a local association asked us to design a communicator for a girl affected by cerebral palsy. There were some portable communicators on the market, but they were very expensive for the family. We developed a less expensive portable communicator called *Lamia*. The two prototypes we developed were quite cheap because we did not charge for labor, R&D equipment, premises, overheads, etc.

The communicator was effective, and the girl, her family and her educators were happy. However, we were frequently required to do minor hardware repairs, software updates, and functionality extensions. Since our main occupation was teaching and research, all these activities had to take place outside of working hours. We found that in addition to designing and developing products, training users and maintaining equipment is critical. We could not replace a company with good customer service - this being one of the reasons for its higher prices.

Since small institutions cannot afford a large marketing and support department, academic research teams use other delivery systems: free software available on the Internet, 3D printable devices, etc. With this model, people with disabilities or their representatives can download advanced interaction systems at no cost. However, this model is only valid if the designers can ensure long-lasting, sustainable and reliable support for their downloadable products for people with disabilities.

> *Trustful Assistive Technology requires guaranties and services that R&D institutions cannot provide. AT final prices cannot be reduced exclusively to the price of the components, not even including the complete R&D process pricing*

For further reading Pino et al. [4] present a comprehensive inventory of Open Source/Freeware Assistive Technology software. An interesting discussion on this topic can be found in Heron et al. [5].

3.2 A Solution in Search of a Problem

Well-disposed technologists envision applications to increase user capacities or find alternatives to lost skills. However, the proposed solutions are not always convenient or accepted by the target users.

Some of our colleagues, members of a reputed R&D team, developed in the 90's an advanced piece of technology, solid and sound. It consisted of a sonar torch for blind people to replace the white cane. They soon discovered that blind users turned down the opportunity to try it because it barely substituted the information provided by the white cane. These users only agreed to test the torch if they were allowed to simultaneously use the white cane (which was meant to be replaced!). We learned from their experience that an accessibility project always requires a previous sound study of user needs in order to be viable.

Fig. 1. A glass of water?

> *User needs cannot be imagined. Only rigorous studies conducted with actual users can provide this information.*

3.3 Technology-Driven Projects

We technologists are excited to apply fashionable technological advancements. We generally have impressive technology at our fingertips and are tempted to use it to develop sophisticated accessibility equipment. This approach frequently leads to solutions that are overly technological or more expensive and complex than necessary. In addition, equipment designed following this approach is often rejected by users because it can make them stand out too much.

I remember reading an excellent paper (from the technological point of view) about an enormous exoskeleton (which gave the user the appearance of a character from the movie Transformers) developed to allow a tetraplegic person to drink from a glass autonomously (Fig. 1).

> *The starting point of an accessibility project must be the solution of a problem. The opposite approach is likely to produce results directly for the storeroom.*

3.4 "Recycled" Research and Development

For many reasons, the money invested in R&D to develop technology for people with disabilities does not appear to produce sufficiently good results for these users. Finding the causes would require an in-depth study encompassing the international assistive technology market, the diverse national social support structures, and the R&D financing schemes.

As a reviewer of research proposals, I have found projects that were clearly recycled from other R&D projects with the only change being the addition to the title of the words "for people with disabilities" or "for elderly people". A colleague reviewer used to call these projects "roller skates for elderly people" (Fig. 2).

On the other hand, in recent years some research institutions seem to have redirected their focus to the areas of Accessibility and eHealth due of the greater availability of subsidies and public funds in this area. Some of them have been successful in this move, but others have not been able to overcome the lack of experience and training in these fields. This may be another reason for their limited innovation and scant contribution to the accessibility area, described by some experts as "variations on the same theme" or "reinventing the wheel".

> *Before starting a research project, it should be verified whether a similar system has been produced before or not. If so, it should be possible to argue that the new proposal is better than the previous ones and why.*

4 Technology vs. Users: This Is Not My Problem

In 2001, I chaired a session at a conference on Digital Accessibility in Slovenia. After a mostly technological presentation made by a brilliant, young speaker, someone asked

Fig. 2. Roller skaters for elderly people.

him a question: "Do you think that your development is usable and accessible for the target population with disabilities you are considering?" His answer was: "I do not know, and I do not care. I am an engineer".

Unfortunately a large number of designers are committed to technology, but not to users. Even if this approach is changing quickly, some people still think that a good technical design is enough for the success of a product, regardless of its suitability for users: if necessary, specialists would add accessibility in the future.

By contrast, people working in Digital Accessibility know that the accessibility barriers included in the initial design can only be removed in future stages of the development with great difficulty.

> *AT designs must be accessible and usable from the conception phase. Accessibility is not something that can be "added" to a non-accessible product.*

5 Who Rules?

Since their advent, portable computers have been viewed as candidates for improving human communication. For this reason, they have been frequently used to create Augmentative and Alternative Communication devices for people with oral communication restrictions. For their part, robotic devices add the possibility of physically interacting with the environment. In the area of accessibility they have been used for physical movement (mainly by means of smart wheelchairs), assisted manipulation (using light articulated arms) and accompaniment and monitoring (for instance by pet-robots). The first two cases require advanced human-robot interfaces in order to be used correctly. Still, users can often experience difficulty in maintaining control.

Fig. 3. Have we forgotten something?

5.1 The Case of Smart Wheelchairs

Almost every Robotics laboratory in the world has developed a smart wheelchair (we have too). These wheelchairs are equipped with state-of-the-art sensors (laser, GPS, video cameras, etc.) and controllers. Actually, they are complex mobile robots able to autonomously drive –or help the user to drive– to a required destination. Most of us have never dared to transfer the design to a company. A colleague of ours did so and was angered because all the companies he contacted rejected the idea of manufacturing his sophisticated smart wheelchair. The companies disputed two main issues: its high price and the difficulty for marketing, training, maintenance, and repairing such a complex piece of equipment.

Wheelchair companies know that in addition to having "reasonable prices", the equipment should be "discrete", and the user interface must be accessible, usable and easy to learn and master.

When it comes to smart wheelchairs, they usually offer high performance as autonomous mobile robots, although human-robot interaction is often problematic. Paradoxically, for these robots the main problem is the user: smart wheelchairs are completely autonomous and do not know how to cope with the "strange being" that sits on them (Fig. 3). The user-wheelchair interface has to solve two main issues: who is in control and how the user and the wheelchair can efficiently communicate.

Fig. 4. The obstacle avoiding system works perfect!

In collaboration with the research group led by Professor Anton Civit (University of Seville) we designed an extremely safe smart wheelchair called TetraNauta [6]. Users who tested it soon discovered that the anti-crash module prevented them from approaching a table, for instance (Fig. 4). In fact, users were not allowed any potentially dangerous movements, which greatly limited their options. We had to redesign the control system applying Shared Control/Mixed Initiative methods. The idea is that both agents (human and wheelchair) collaborate to make decisions, and assume full control when necessary. To this end, both of them need to know the other agent's abilities (through a partner's mental model) and to be able to negotiate disagreements. To facilitate efficient communication we designed an adaptive smart user interface based on user/context/task models.

5.2 The Case of Assisted Manipulation with Articulated Arms

Lightweight articulated arms can be installed on wheelchairs, beds or desks. They are useful to help people with motor restrictions in their upper extremities to manipulate everyday objects. Since these robots operate in 3D environments, they require information on the position (x, y, z coordinates) and the orientation (α, β, γ angles) of the object to be handed. As users are unaware of the exact coordinates, they cannot provide them. Even if they were known, selecting six data items for one move would become tedious. Machine Vision technics may help to find and locate familiar objects, making commands like "bring me that glass" easier. However, complex user interfaces are still required to allow the user the vast number of possibilities that an articulated arm offers. These interfaces can reduce the complexity of the command taking into account the context of use and the user preferences and habits.

5.3   Importance of the User Interface

Advanced equipment usually incorporates a plethora of functions and commands. Interfaces that just present them to the user tend to be complex and difficult to be learned and used. For some users multiple selections imply an extra physical or cognitive effort that may prevent them from benefiting from the proper functionality [7] (Fig. 5).

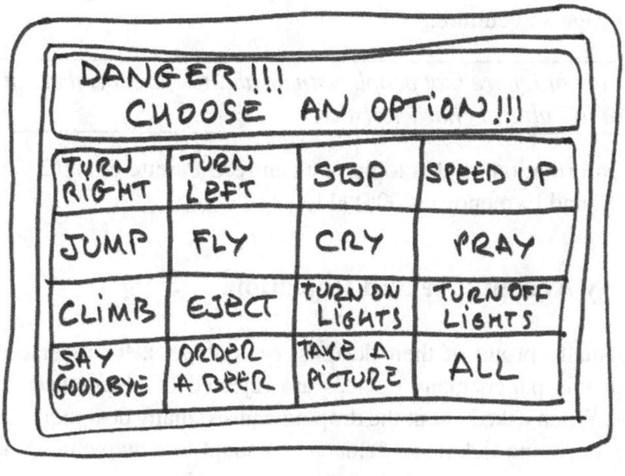

Fig. 5. You have to make a quick choice!

Human-Computer Interaction theories and procedures are applied to develop smart user interfaces that make it easier for users to perform selections taking into account their past choices, the environment, the task at hand, etc. Adaptive user interfaces based on user, context and task models are often suitable for this purpose.

> *Since Robotics has historically focused on the design of autonomous systems, there is the possibility that users are excluded from the assistance provided by robotic systems.*

Keates and Kyberd (2017) [8] discuss this issue and present possible ways forward to ensure that the next generation robots support the principles of universal access.

6   Cultural Barriers to Assistive Technology

The cultural background of AT users (and their social context) influence the success or failure of AT acceptance/rejection. The users' native culture, language, beliefs, and customs must be taken into account. To compel people to acquire and try to use technology that they do not understand, do not believe in or cannot accept leads to AT failure. Matching even the best, most complex, and most expensive high-tech AT with users who are culturally unprepared or unwilling to accept and use such devices will still result in AT failure.

CHAT was a pioneer Augmentative and Alternative Communication system to help people with severe communication restrictions. It was developed in the 90 s by the team lead by Professor Alan Newell (an AT pioneer) at the University of Dundee Microcenter. Basically, it consisted of a set of pre-programmed sentences and words, structured by a model that considered diverse aspects, such as environment, mood, phase of the conversation, etc. We were allowed to translate it from English to the Basque language. The first Basque version did not work well because we maintained the British model of the dialogue. We ignored the importance of context, for instance in the small talk and good-bye phases. The system was acceptable only after adapting the conversation model to the local language and culture.

> *Designers cannot ignore that people with disabilities are members of a society and share its cultural characteristics.*

For further information on this topic you can read Parette et al. (2004) [9], Parette et al. (2005) [10], and Evmenova (2005) [11].

7   Technology Acceptance and Rejection

Designers are usually proud of their designs. Nevertheless, for diverse reasons mentioned earlier in this paper, many devices are rejected or abandoned early by users with disabilities. When asked about the dropout causes, many designers seem upset and blame the users for being fickle and reluctant to adapt to new technologies. However, our experience working with users is just the opposite. Users are generally adaptive and tolerant with our "crazy prototypes" and they love innovations that help them to be more autonomous. When rejection occurs, the reasons are obvious if we ask the users:

- Greater effort: often due to the complexity of the user interface, some equipment increases the effort required from the user to produce an output similar to the one produced by themselves.
- Tagging users: some equipment makes disability more noticeable, making social integration more difficult. Users tend to prefer discrete devices.
- Misrepresenting users: some equipment provides user representation to other people, especially an image or a voice. Users tend to reject equipment that clearly differs from their own personality.

The rejection and abandonment of Assistive Technology is a complex problem that can have multiple causes. For more information read Phillips and Zhao [12].

In 1998 I stayed at Loughborough University working with Colette Nicolle on a book on the use of guidelines for accessible design [13]. That work inspired us to subsequently research and write a paper on social and ethical issues related to assistive technology design [14]. As we collected examples of assistive technology abandonment for that work, we were informally told about an issue with one of the early text-to-voice Augmentative and Alternative Communication systems. This communicator spoke each sentence written in a small computer by means of an adapted input system in fairly clear English. The device was loaned to a 12-year-old girl with cerebral palsy for testing. The designers could not believe that she refused to use it at the school. Asked for the reason behind her rejection the girl replied she did not want to speak like a 30-year-old male robot. The designers knew that the voice was quite strange, but their argument was "Isn't a male robot voice better than nothing?" Obviously, most users think that it is not the case.

> Users with disabilities have their own opinions, feelings and desires, which designers must understand and respect.

8 Deceptive Diffusion of Results

A metric for the quality of the research are publications in sound scientific journals. Research institutions also promote public dissemination of their results in public media (TV, newspapers, etc.). The information that reaches the public is not always completely reliable as some journalists prefer striking headlines, others misinterpret important details or simply because the researchers are not completely clear.

I usually follow internet channels reporting advances in Digital Accessibility and Assistive Technology. According to numerous headlines, most of the restrictions and barriers experienced by people with disabilities have already been overcome by new technological advances: "Quadriplegic people drive wheelchairs with their minds", "Implanted integrated circuit returns sight to blind people", "Hundreds of children regain manipulative capacity using 3D printed prosthetic arms",...

If you go to the small print, if there is any, many of these are early stage projects, or they have been tested with non-disabled people in very specific environments, for short periods...

In 1994 we organized a Summer School on "Design of Human-Computer Interfaces for Disabled People" supported by the European Community. We were honored by the participation of four prestigious professors: Arthur Karshmer, Rick Kazman, Alfred Kobsa, and Angel Puerta. The course was particularly successful. However, I cannot forget a sad story. During the presentation of the course to the press, one of the presenters mentioned that in the future (we were in 1994) amputees could use bionic hands. A newspaper chain published the headline that the professors on the course had designed bionic hands for amputees. The next day, a family from a distant city waited at the front of the classroom before the beginning of the first lesson. They wanted to buy a bionic hand for their amputee child.

> Researchers are responsible for the veracity of information disseminated about their work and must verify all the data before publication. In such a sensitive field misleading information can harm people.

9 "Universal" as a Synecdoche

According to the Collins Dictionary[3] "synecdoche is a figure of speech in which a part is substituted for a whole or a whole for a part". I wonder if the word "Universal" included in the expression "Universal Accessibility" can be considered a synecdoche. Universal means "for all" but it refers in this context to only a small part of the population. These are the people that can afford the equipment required to achieve accessibility. Nevertheless, the majority of the world's disabled population cannot benefit from technology "designed for everyone". Is this the goal of Universal Accessibility? [15].

Let's admit that when technologists say "Universal" they mean digital technology that can be used by "anyone regardless of their physical, sensory or cognitive condition". However, in addition to disability, other barriers can hinder access to the equipment required for accessibility. Some of these barriers, such as economic ones, can only be removed through appropriate local social policies and international collaboration with developing countries. However, designers are also responsible for removing certain barriers they have (probably inadvertently) included in their designs. They should bear in mind that to be universal, accessibility technology must be robust, durable, inexpensive, and not require complex technological environments, such as fast network connectivity or expensive software [16].

> All accessibility-related projects should consider non-technological issues, such as the final price, technology requirements, and the impact on security and privacy.

10 User Testing Without Users

The ultimate way to validate a product with people with disabilities is formal user testing with appropriate user samples. Most serious journals and conferences require this kind of validation. However, they are often performed with people without disabilities (sometimes artificially placed in disability conditions). Even when real users are recruited, it often happens that representative samples of users are not selected, no real conditions are deployed, no real tasks are allocated, etc. Sometimes, insufficient planning leads to inadequate hypotheses and insufficient evidence. Thus, the evaluations cannot draw conclusions about the accessibility and usability of the product, but rather about other characteristics.

It is evident, for example, that people wearing masks that cover their eyes cannot substitute blind people in tests because they have different perception systems, mental models and user strategies. However, some people still think that they can test accessibility to a website for visually impaired people just by switching-off the screen (Fig. 6).

---

[3] Collins Concise English Dictionary © HarperCollins Publishers

Fig. 6. Pretending

Students are easily accessed by academic researchers. They are abundant and enthusiastic to participate in prototype testing, especially if they are rewarded. The results of these tests may be valid for an initial idea of the suitability of the product, but can they be used to support accessibility or usability?

In 1994 I was invited to give a talk in a conference in Austria where another speaker presented an ingenious Augmentative and Alternative Communication system. A screenless communicator that spoke texts put together by selecting from among 64 words or letters, if I remember correctly. A device with a small number of buttons, located in the user's pocket, was used to select each item by means of a series of key combinations. The selectable items were mentally represented as living in a 4-story house for easy recall. For instance, the first code was used to select the floor (from 1st to 4th), the second one to select the room (one of four) and the third one to select 1 out of 4 items (sentences, words or letters) in that room. The user only needed to remember where each element lived to form the codes (without looking at the keys). This system was designed for people with severe communication restrictions and was tested by motivated engineering students. The test was reported to be successful: students were able to memorize the usage in under two hours. I wonder if it was possible to extrapolate these results to people with communication disabilities.

> *Only people with disabilities can assess the accessibility and usability of the AT designed for them.*

11   Knowing the Users

One of the main causes of R&D failures in accessibility is the lack of awareness of the characteristics of the users with disabilities. Many pioneers of digital accessibility became involved in this field because they, or a relative of theirs, had a disability. Therefore, they had direct knowledge of the capacities, interests, likes and restrictions of users with specific disabilities. When the field of Digital Accessibility was extended, the direct relation with the users declined. Currently, few researchers personally know any user, or they have very superficial relationships with them. For this reason, they often do not know how to treat the users or communicate with users. They may even "be afraid" of the users.

Once able to overcome communication barriers, accessibility engineers may discover that people with disabilities are "normal people" who share similar interests and concerns with the entire population. Therefore, it is crucial that researchers receive training about disability and learn how to deal with and communicate properly with these users.

Between 2019 and 2011, our laboratory was subcontracted by a large national accessibility project carried out by 14 industries. We developed an automated generator of accessible and adaptable user interfaces for ubiquitous services. Working under the control of a company was stressful and, due to time constraints, we were unable to test various design alternatives. Some of the team members hired for that project never had direct contact with the users. After concluding the project, our team used the remaining funds to try our own approach and test it with users. When our version of the UI generator, called Egoki [17], was finished, these young researchers reported that they were happy to have been able to contribute with new ideas, but they were especially happy to have been able to discuss and test the prototypes with people with disabilities. They were even angry with me for the time spent without knowing the users!

> *Interaction with users with disabilities greatly facilitates the design, development and evaluation of accessibility projects and often provides motivation for designers.*

12 Conclusion

Most design failures derive from a misconception of the user needs, their characteristics and their desires.

Users with disabilities are true experts in their own restrictions. They have long experience in developing strategies to negotiate them. A decisive condition for success is asking them to participate from the early stages of R&D projects. Participatory Design is an increasingly popular methodology for including users in design decisions. Obviously, the participation of users require the establishment of adequate participation channels, to prevent other participants from patronizing them or ignoring their opinions [18].

It is universally accepted that basic research is fundamental to the advancement of science. However, there exist research projects supported by accessibility funds that carry out basic research with low expected impact in accessibility that, in the future, would be applicable to other diverse technological fields. Taking into account the priorities of people with disabilities in the short and medium term, it is ethically challenging to use these funds for research that is not specifically devoted to their needs.

Funds for accessibility research should be primarily applied to questions not normally investigated in other scientific fields.

Acknowledgments. The author is the head of the EGOKITUZ/ADIAN research team, supported by the Basque Government, Department of Education, Universities and Research under grant IT980-16, and participates in the PhysCom project, funded by the Spanish Ministry of Economy and Competitiveness and the European Regional Development Fund (grant TIN2017-85409-P).

References

1. Hoare C.A.R.: The emperor's old clothes. In: The 1980 ACM Turing Award Lecture (1981). Commun. ACM **24**(2), 75–83
2. Keates, S., Kyberd, P.: Robotic assistants for universal access. In: Antona, M., Stephanidis, C. (eds.) UAHCI 2017. LNCS, vol. 10279, pp. 527–538. Springer, Cham (2017). https://doi.org/10.1007/978-3-319-58700-4_43
3. Abascal, J.G., Gardeazabal, L., Arruabarrena, A.: Providing telecommunications access to people with special needs. IEEE J. Sel. Areas Commun. **9**(4), 601–604 (1991)
4. Pino, A., Kouroupetroglou, G., Kacorri, H., Sarantidou, A., Spiliotopoulos, D.: An open source/freeware assistive technology software inventory. In: Miesenberger, K., Klaus, J., Zagler, W., Karshmer, A. (eds.) ICCHP 2010. LNCS, vol. 6179, pp. 178–185. Springer, Heidelberg (2010). https://doi.org/10.1007/978-3-642-14097-6_29
5. Heron, M., Hanson, V., Ricketts, I.: Open source and accessibility: advantages and limitations. J. Interact. Sci. **1**, 1–10 (2013)
6. Vicente Diaz, S., Amaya Rodriguez, C., Diaz del Rio, F., Civit Balcells, A., Cagigas Muniz, D.: TetraNauta: an intelligent wheelchair for users with very severe mobility restrictions. In: Proceedings of the International Conference on Control Applications, Glasgow, vol. 2, pp. 778–783 (2002)
7. Abascal, J.: Users with disabilities: maximum control with minimum effort. In: Perales, F.J., Fisher, R.B. (eds.) AMDO 2008. LNCS, vol. 5098, pp. 449–456. Springer, Heidelberg (2008). https://doi.org/10.1007/978-3-540-70517-8_44
8. Keates, S., Kyberd, P.: Robotic assistants for universal access. In: Antona, M., Stephanidis, C. (eds.) UAHCI 2017. LNCS, vol. 10279, pp. 527–538. Springer, Cham (2017). https://doi.org/10.1007/978-3-319-58700-4_43
9. Parette, H.P., Blake Huer, M., Scherer, M.: Effects of acculturation on assistive technology service delivery. J. Spec. Educ. Technol. **19**(2), 31–41 (2004)
10. Parette, H.P., Breslin Larson, J.: Family and cultural issues in assistive technology, 2. Faculty Publications - College of Education (2005). https://ir.library.illinoisstate.edu/fped/2
11. Evmenova, A.: Cultural barriers to assistive technology. SPED 6701. East Carolina University (2005)
12. Phillips, B., Zhao, H.: Predictors of assistive technology abandonment. Assistive Technol. **5**(1), 36–45 (1993)
13. Nicolle, C., Abascal, J. (eds.): Inclusive Design Guidelines for HCI. Taylor & Francis, London (2001)
14. Abascal, J., Nicolle, C.: Moving towards inclusive design guidelines for socially and ethically aware HCI. Interact. Comput. **17**(5), 484–505 (2005)
15. Abascal, J., Barbosa, S.D.J., Nicolle, C., Zaphiris, P.: Rethinking universal accessibility: a broader approach considering the digital gap. Univ. Access Inf. Soc. **15**(2), 179–182 (2015). https://doi.org/10.1007/s10209-015-0416-1
16. Abascal, J., Azevedo, L., Cook, A.: Is universal accessibility on track? In: Antona, M., Stephanidis, C. (eds.) UAHCI 2016. LNCS, vol. 9737, pp. 135–143. Springer, Cham (2016). https://doi.org/10.1007/978-3-319-40250-5_13

17. Gamecho, B., et al.: Automatic generation of tailored accessible user interfaces for ubiquitous services. IEEE Trans. Hum. Mach. Syst. **45**(5), 612–623 (2015)
18. Abascal, J., Arrue, M., Pérez, J.E.: Applying participatory design with users with intellectual disabilities. In: Loizides, et al. (eds.) Human Computer Interaction and Emerging Technologies: Adjunct Proceedings from the INTERACT 2019 Workshops, pp. 321–326. Cardiff University Press, Cardiff (2020)

Empowering Citizen-Environment Interaction vs. Importunate Computer-Dominated Interaction: Let's Reset the Priorities!

Norbert A. Streitz(✉) ⓘ

Smart Future Initiative, 60438 Frankfurt, Germany
norbert.streitz@smart-future.net

Abstract. This paper starts out by extending the scope of traditional human-computer interaction research towards human-*environment* interaction and in the context of smart cities to *citizen-environment* interaction. This is complemented by a critical evaluation of technology-driven approaches in the development and deployment of smart environments, especially for smart cities. It argues to reset the priorities by putting humans and citizens first and computer technologies with non-transparent AI-based mechanisms second in contrast to current developments resulting in increased automation in all kinds of applications. The evaluation of this 'smart-everything paradigm' implies to reflect and to redefine the basic assumptions. Based on the concept of 'human-technology symbiosis', the paper discusses several design trade-offs as, e.g., 'human control and empowerment vs. automated and autonomous systems' and 'usable privacy vs. importunate smartness'. The resulting proposal for urban environments is to move beyond 'smart-only' cities and to establish the goal of humane, sociable, and cooperative hybrid cities, reconciling people and technology by providing a balance between human control and automation as well as privacy and smartness. This can be achieved by viewing the city and its citizens as mutual cooperation partners, where a city is 'smart' in the sense of being 'self-aware' and 'cooperative' towards its citizens by supporting them in their activities. The goal is to enable citizens to exploit their individual, creative, social, and economic potential and to live a self-determined life, thus meeting some of the challenges of the urban age by enabling people to experience and enjoy a satisfying life and work.

Keywords: Human-Computer Interaction · Human-Environment Interaction · Citizen-Environment Interaction · Smart City · Smart-Only City · Hybrid City · Cooperative City · Self-Aware City · Urban Age · Smart-Everything Paradigm · Citizen-Centered Design · Design Trade-Offs · Human-in-the-Loop · Human in Control · Human Empowerment · Smartness · Privacy · Privacy by Design · Ethical · Human-Technology Symbiosis · Automated Driving · Autonomous Systems · Artificial Intelligence · Non-Transparent AI · Ambient Intelligence · Disappearing Computer · Ubiquitous Computing

1 Introduction

One of the initial main conferences in the area was the 'Human Factors in Computer Systems' conference in Gaithersburg, Maryland, US, in 1982. At this meeting, the ACM

© Springer Nature Switzerland AG 2021
M. J. Escalona et al. (Eds.): CHIRA 2018/CHIRA 2019, CCIS 1351, pp. 41–59, 2021.
https://doi.org/10.1007/978-3-030-67108-2_3

Special Interest Group on Computer–Human Interaction (SIGCHI) was first publicly announced. This led to the acronym 'CHI' for this conference series, standing for '*Computer*-Human Interaction'. It might seem like a marginal observation, but here 'computer' was put first and 'human' second, although the initial long name put 'human factors' first and 'computing systems' second. The general field of research was called '*Human*-Computer Interaction' reflecting the priorities I also like to emphasize in this paper. In addition, I will extend the scope of interaction to the new challenges we are facing by living in and interacting with smart environments by not only being 'users' but 'citizens' of the urban environment we inhabit. This perspective was also contributed to a larger team effort, elaborated and described in a survey article [27], where we identified the following Seven Grand Challenges: 1) Human-Technology Symbiosis, 2) Human-Environment Interactions, 3) Ethics, Privacy and Security, 4) Well-being, Health and Eudaimonia, 5) Accessibility and Universal Access, 6) Learning and Creativity, and 7) Social Organization and Democracy. Since there is obviously not enough space to cover all of them here, I will mainly focus on issues related to human-technology symbiosis, human-environment interactions, and privacy as well as ethics.

There was and in many research and development communities still is the predominant opinion that humans should be in control of their interactions with computer-based technologies, functionalities, and services, ubiquitously available and supposedly making our lives easier. But there is also an increasing tendency towards automation and in many cases non-transparent systems-based control of our activities. Thus, it seems that the 'computer' is again being put first by many people. This paper is meant to propagate a user-/citizen-centered design approach that puts humans first again, thus resetting the priorities.

At the early times, the typical usage scenario to be investigated was: one person sitting in front of a 'video display terminal' (VDT) [5] and interacting with the underlying system by using command languages (see also Fig. 1 - left). The computer system dominated the options available in a strict fashion. Human factors and cognitive ergonomics research in the 80ies (e.g., [4, 23, 28, 29] and many others) proposed and realized to make the interaction more 'user-friendly' so that also non-computer experts could use computers. The usage paradigm at those times was the "*one user - one device to interact with*" situation, being dominant for several decades. But it should be obvious to go beyond this simple set of scenarios and look much more at the different contexts where interactions of (many) people with (multiple) computers, devices or rather technology-augmented environments in general are happening. Instead of dealing with individual, often personal desk-top computers, laptops, tablets, smartphones, etc., experiences and interactions of humans with 'computers' are and will increasingly take place in the context of interacting with 'smart artefacts', embedded and integrated into the environment and in a next phase with 'smart materials' constituting 'smart ecosystems' [35, 39]. There can be no doubt, that this has serious implications for the future of the field currently still called 'human-computer-interaction'.

The other aspect, i.e., "*many people with multiple computers/devices*" was addressed early by research on Computer-Supported Cooperative Work (CSCW). A good overview over the early work was provided by Greif [13]. This was at a time, when the support of local and/or distributed collaborative teams was enabled already before the World Wide

© Norbert Streitz

Fig. 1. Historical development of configurations how humans interact with computers (from left to right). The left illustration shows one person in front of a desktop computer with a separate monitor. The center illustration shows 'computers' and displays getting closer to the human body, eventually merging with the body. The right illustration shows a human in a connected smart building surrounded by smart devices, monitoring and controlling activities, functionalities, and the physical space. Thus, the human has moved somehow 'inside' the 'computer artefact'.

Web (WWW) was invented and applications integrated web-based services. Examples are support for groups engaged in creating shared hypermedia documents [41] or brainstorming meetings [20, 42, 49], support for collaborative work between distributed governments [14] and support for virtual organizations [16]. These are all scenarios, that currently - in the context of the Corona-Virus situation - are gaining again more and more interest.

With the development of the WWW, web-based solutions conquered a wide range of application domains. Providing support for 'multiple people' interaction and communication, resulted in 'social media' applications with all their benefits and serious problems at the same time. In parallel, there was a transfer from desk-top computers and laptops to other types of devices resulting in 'mobile applications' running on tablets, smart phones, smart watches, etc. As a side effect, basically every application software is now called an 'app', whatever the point of that may be.

1.1 Three Focal Points of This Paper

The overall guiding motivation results in three main lines of arguments and approaches presented in this paper, but they are not independent of each other.

As outlined above, computers were initially large or medium-size artefacts filling the whole room or sitting in the corner of a room operated from a separate control desk. Later, they were placed under the table with keyboards and displays on the desktop in front of us (Fig. 1 - left). But computers and devices became smaller and lighter so that they could be placed on our laps ('laptops') and became portable. The next major development step resulted in devices not looking like computers anymore by becoming even smaller and very close to us, as handhelds and wearables and attached to various parts of our body or even implanted inside of us, monitoring all kinds of our activities (Fig. 1 - center). With a different objective, but more or less in parallel, large physical artefacts like cars, homes, office buildings, shopping centers and even airports were turned into smart artefacts and environments where almost the complete functionality is computer-enabled and controlled. Here, we are now surrounded by or embedded in a large comprehensive smart computing environment controlled by hardware and software. The connected smart building decides if we can enter or leave our house, the smart (autonomous) car determines where to go and which route to take, etc. One can argue that when riding a smart car, we are just inside a large (mobile) computer on wheels and when residing in a smart building we are inside a large stationary computer (Fig. 1 – right).

One could also view smart cars and smart buildings or, in general, 'smart spaces' as large 'robots' surrounding passengers and inhabitants. These smart spaces are to be considered as a compound physical agent that acquires data from its environment through sensors and acts upon it via actuators. Contrary to a 'classical robot' that operates towards its outside, the cognitive capabilities of a smart space can be considered as an 'outside-in robot' [51], where the human inside is a constitutive element of the smart environment and as such is sensed and acted upon by the space. As smart spaces scale up, they may also comprise nested smart spaces such as a smart building being composed of several smart rooms.

The next level of aggregating smart spaces is the 'smart city'. The term refers to the deployment of information and communication technology (ICT) as infrastructure for realizing future cities providing smart services [3]. For a detailed discussion of different 'smart city' terminologies see [39]. Whatever terminology is used, there is no doubt, that the 'smart city' constitutes a so far unknown comprehensive computerized living envelope or huge and massive 'robot' in an unprecedented way. We come back to the discussion of the main challenges related to it.

The developments illustrated above result in at least three focal points to be discussed in this paper:

1) The first focus results from the historical development of how people interact with computing systems as briefly described and illustrated above. It implies that we must shift from the traditional 'Human-Computer Interaction' (HCI) perspective to a more comprehensive 'Human-Environment Interaction' (HEI) perspective [32]. Related areas of research are Ambient Intelligence and the Disappearing Computer.

2) The second focus is motivated by the observation that our living, working, and computing environments are being determined by what I call the 'smart-everything paradigm' [39]. Every artefact and every service must be 'smart' – whatever it means – so that 'smart' became the buzzword of our times. Unfortunately, the corresponding developments are based on primarily technology-driven approaches. When looking closer at the associated challenges and concerns, we need considering design trade-offs on various dimensions. In this paper, I will focus especially on two trade-offs: 'human control and empowerment vs. automated and autonomous systems' and 'usable privacy vs. importunate smartness'. The overall design should be guided by the goal of 'human-technology symbiosis'.

3) The third focus is based on the observation that the technology-driven approaches are hyped especially in the areas of 'smart cities' and 'autonomous vehicles.' The increasing relevance of people's interactions in smart urban environments must be

considered when designing current and future cities constituting the Urban Age. The more we seem to be at the mercy of computers and their system developers, the more important it is therefore to focus on the needs and concerns of us as 'citizens'. Our views and participation in such design contexts must be reflected in a shift from HCI and HEI towards '*Citizen*-Environment Interaction' (CEI) [38]. This includes participatory design and other approaches to ward off current developments towards computer-dominated environments controlled by - often non-transparent - artificial intelligence and machine learning algorithms, removing human control and infringing people's privacy in current and future smart urban environments.

2 Shifting Towards Human-*Environment* Interaction (HEI)

The first focus of this paper concerns the shift of human-*computer* interaction towards human-*environment* interaction (HEI). It is motivated by technical as well as application developments and was proposed in 2006 by Streitz [32] based on experimental developments, especially in the area of ambient intelligence (AmI) and the disappearing computer, at that time. The technical developments can be roughly described in terms of an increasing number of sensors and actuators attached to real-world objects, constituting smart artefacts. Once they are not only distributed in the physical environment, but also connected, they form a networked smart environment, often labeled as the Internet of Things (IoT). While this approach is very much based on individual sensors and actuators, Streitz [35, 38, 39] predicts a shift towards a computing, communication, sensing and interaction 'substrate', which can be handled at the application or domain level. It is realized via 'smart materials' constituting 'smart ecosystems'. Indoor examples are smart tablecloth, smart wall-paper and smart paint. Out-door, one will find smart street-surfaces, building façades, windows as well as large wall-type public displays. All of them require a seamless integration of smart material components with a high degree of diffusion leading to an emergent smartness of the overall environment. This smart ecosystem might soon parallel other existing ecosystems.

At the same time, current and future application developments are focusing on the instrumentation of urban environments and provision of services in public spaces beyond buildings as well as the facilitation of automated driving with smart cars. This requires an extended perspective of interaction, because people do not interact anymore with a small set of usually personal devices, but with a comprehensive smart environment in an often not very transparent way.

Based on existing developments as well as predictions, it is inevitable to rethink the basics of interacting with 'computing devices'. In the envisioned ubiquitous smart ecosystems, the computer disappears as a 'visible' distinctive device, either physically due to being integrated in the environment or mentally from our perception [31, 33]. It is also the core of the 'Disappearing Computer' (DC) approach [26, 45] and is very well illustrated by the following quote from Streitz and Nixon [46]: "*It seems like a paradox but it will soon become reality: The rate at which computers disappear will be matched by the rate at which information technology will increasingly permeate our environment and our lives*". For detailed descriptions of the research efforts investigating a wide range of DC issues, carried out by sixteen projects of 'The Disappearing Computer Initiative', funded by the European Commission in the Future and Emerging Technology (FET) program, see the corresponding DC survey book [45].

There are a number of challenges associated with this approach, e.g., the circumstance that 'users' are in many cases not anymore fully aware of the interaction options they are provided with in their current smart environments. Another related issue is that they receive no feedback about wrong or inadequate user input or even system failures. The design challenge is how to communicate the actions and interactions possible in the respective environment when one cannot rely anymore on the traditional types of 'affordances' as proposed by Gibson [11, 12] and discussed by Norman [21, 22]. The properties of ambient intelligent environments require therefore to rethink the notion of affordances [40]. Streitz et al. [47] proposed the notion of 'inherited affordances' providing new 'clues' when considering integrated smart environments, e.g., so called *Roomware®*[1] environments [43, 44, 52], i.e., the integration of room elements like tables, lecterns, chairs, walls, doors, etc. with smart technologies. For completeness, it must be noted here that the 'disappearance' feature has also serious implications for privacy issues (e.g., lack of information what kind of sensors are distributed in the environment monitoring activities), to be discussed in more detail in Sect. 4.2.

Furthermore, another related approach must be mentioned in this context: *Ambient Intelligence* (AmI) was created in the late 1990s in the context of activities initiated by Philips[2] and prominently publicized by Emile Aarts. In addition, it became known via the activities of the IST Advisory Group (ISTAG) of the European Commission [15]. AmI is building on the ideas of Ubiquitous Computing proposed by Mark Weiser around 1990 at Xerox PARC and communicated to the scientific community in his seminal article in Scientific American [53]. Although Weiser addressed with his proposal of a 'calm technology' also the relationship of ubiquitous technologies and the perception and behavior of people, most of the follow-up research in ubiquitous computing took a rather technology-driven route. In contrast, the AmI proposal promotes an approach with a more elaborated emphasis on user-oriented design, the human perspective in general as well as on the social context addressed by social interfaces. Examples of the Ambient Intelligence approach were realized in the 'Ambient Agoras' project [24, 47, 50] in the context of facilitating communication and collaboration in office buildings or in the domain of pervasive game applications [19]. Many of the now intensively discussed relationships between Ubiquitous Computing, Internet of Things, Disappearing Computer, Artificial Intelligence and Ambient Intelligence were described and investigated in a comprehensive book chapter by Streitz and Privat [48].

3 Issues and Challenges of the Smart-Everything Paradigm

The second focus of this paper addresses a more general problem we are already now confronted with and will be even more in the future. This discussion must be taken to a more general level concerning the functioning of our society and the well-being of its citizens. Our society, especially in its urban and global context is already confronted

---

[1] Roomware® was trademarked by Norbert Streitz.
[2] For a description of the history of AmI see Aarts and Encarnacao [1].

with many dependencies, e.g., secure availability of electricity (danger of blackouts) and reliable functioning of 'traditional' software and infrastructure platforms. In the not so far future, we will also be dependent on ubiquitous and pervasive infrastructures providing 'smart' services in many areas of our daily life. We see the beginnings in 'smart homes', 'smart cars', 'smart cities'. Everything must be 'smart'. It is a self-reinforcing trend resulting from the combination of different developments like Internet of Things (IoT) and Artificial Intelligence (AI). It includes a shift towards substantial partial or even full automation of activities and services which used to be controlled by human operators. They will be more and more controlled by AI-based algorithms, which are often non-transparent and not traceable. This is reason enough to reflect on the underlying rationale and challenges associated with what Streitz [37, 39] calls the 'smart-everything paradigm'.

Since there is no space here to describe the concerns and considerations in detail, only selected challenges will be mentioned. One challenge is to investigate the approaches and results of AI methods (which in many cases is 'only' machine learning) and put them into perspective. Streitz [39] identified three problem sets of AI and described examples for each set: a) Inability and error-prone behavior, b) Rigidity, and c) Missing transparency, traceability, and accountability. The common learning of investigating these three problem sets is, that the claims and high expectations about AI are fueled by venture capitalists and stakeholders with vested interests although progress is limited. It seems that we experience again an instantiation of the Gartner Hype Cycle ('peak of inflated expectations' followed by a 'through of disillusionment'). There is even the danger, that we will experience another 'AI winter' as in the 1980ies and 1990ies [6]. For the role of AI, it is also important to mention the report of the AI NOW institute at NYU providing recommendations for how to address the issues of missing transparency of AI-based algorithms based on a critical reflection of AI 'black boxes' approaches [2].

4   Human-Technology Symbiosis and Design Trade-Offs

The challenge is now how to cope with the undesired implications of the 'smart-everything paradigm'. In our recent team effort survey article [27] mentioned above, we identified '*human-technology symbiosis*' as a major concept guiding the understanding as well as influencing the design of human-environment interaction and human-technology systems in general. Human-technology symbiosis (based on the Greek word '*symbiosis*' for '*to live together*') refers to defining how humans will live and work harmoniously, cooperatively, and respectfully together with technology. It is an appropriate concept when discussing not only the challenges but also the goals for designing the interactions and co-existence of humans in smart environments, in general, and between citizens and smart cities in particular. The notion of symbiosis is also well supported by the view that the relationship between humans and smart environments should be designed as mutual cooperation partners, where the environment supports humans in their activities in a cooperative fashion as proposed earlier, e.g., via our concept of 'cooperative buildings' [43] and at a larger scale via the *Citizen ⟺ Cooperative City Contract* (CCCC or C4) as proposed by Streitz [39].

When designing systems in general and information technology in particular, one is always confronted with a variety of goals, values, constraints and thus options, that transform the design effort into a problem that does not have one unique solution. There exist rather a range of features and properties to be accounted for, but usually it is not possible to cover all of them at the same time integrated in one result or product. One can realize one alternative which is desirable in exchange for sacrificing something else, because there is a limiting factor. The underlying mechanisms to deal with this kind of ill-defined problems are 'design trade-offs'.

In the next two sections, I present two design trade-offs, addressing the pressing issue of coping with the severe implications of the 'smart-everything paradigm' in terms of 'human control and empowerment vs. automated and autonomous systems' and 'usable privacy vs. importunate smartness', The concept of human-technology symbiosis provides a good basis and value system for the decisions to be made.

4.1 Design Trade-Off: Human Control and Empowerment vs. Automated and Autonomous Systems

The first design trade-off concerns the current shift towards more or even complete automation of previously human operator-controlled activities. Smart devices and underlying algorithms are gaining ground in controlling processes, services, and devices as well as the interaction between devices and humans. Humans are increasingly removed from being the operator, supervisor or at least being in charge and thus from being in control. Therefore, we must reflect on how much control people have over the actual realization of a smart service. Are they still in control to determine how the smart service is provided and under which conditions? Can they still intervene, take control and regulate or even stop the smart service or are they confronted with an automatic system behavior with almost no option for human intervention?

An environment can be considered 'smart', if it enables certain self-directed (re)actions of individual artefacts or ensembles of artefacts based on continuously collected information about the artefacts and the people involved, their activities and the overall context. For example, a space can be 'smart' by storing and exploiting knowledge about which people and artefacts are currently situated within its area, who and what was there before, when and how long, and what kind of activities took place [50]. In addition, this environment could be equipped with smart materials as described before constituting smart ecosystems facilitating some of these features.

Streitz [39, 50] proposed to contrast a 'system-oriented, importunate smartness' approach with a 'people-empowering smartness' approach. These two types of smartness might not exist in their pure and distinct manifestations. They rather represent the end points on a dimension where weighted combinations of both are employed. The design goal is now to accomplish a balance between keeping the human in the loop and in control vs. automated system behavior, in many cases even autonomous behavior, as it is planned for autonomous vehicles and other autonomous robots or drones. Thus, one is confronted with a design trade-off between 'human control and empowerment vs. system automation' as illustrated in Fig. 2 [taken from 39].

One could restate 'being in control' by saying that 'people should own the loop'. The major requirement is that people are empowered by being in control and are not at the mercy of an automated system. This approach can be extended and summarized under the headline 'smart spaces make people smarter'. Beyond owning the loop and being

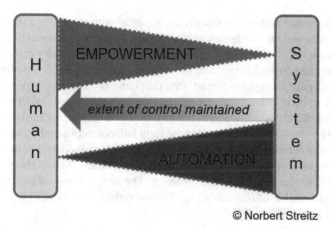

© Norbert Streitz

Fig. 2. Realizing Human-Technology Symbiosis via design trade-offs between human empowerment and system automation depending on the extent of human control maintained.

in control, an empowering function is proposed. It is achieved by providing information and facilitating conditions for making informed decisions and taking actions as mature and responsible people who are in control. In this approach, sensors in the environment will also collect data about what is going on and aggregate them up to a certain level. Important is now, that the space does not operate automatically or autonomously, but communicates the resulting information as guidance for subsequent actions, which are still determined by a person. In this case, a smart space or system makes suggestions and recommendations based on the information collected, but humans still have the final say and make the decision. The space supports and enables smart behavior of people. This type of approach is getting popular as work on soft actuation [8] and citizen actuation [7] in smart environments shows. The people-oriented, empowering smartness approach is in line with the objectives of the Ambient Intelligence approach presented before [48].

The important aspect is that the design trade-off should not be a fixed decision made by a system designer, who determines where on the balance, resp. trade-off dimension a system is to be positioned. System design should allow for flexibility and rather make possible variations accessible under the control of the user. And exactly here, we are again confronted with another challenge, i.e., how to provide and present this control to the users so that they can oversee the interaction. It is one more challenge for future human-environment interaction to provide appropriate affordances for a transparent presentation of the decision and control options and their implications.

4.2 Design-Trade-Off: Usable Privacy vs. Importunate Smartness

The second design trade-off concerns the conflicting goals of assuring privacy vs. exploiting personal data when providing smartness. When being asked, most people will agree that privacy is an important aspect of our everyday life. But when we look at our digital activities as, e.g., in social communities, during on-line shopping, and when using location-based smart services, privacy is very often compromised [36].

Obviously, a smart system can usually be 'smarter' with respect to a service offered if it has more data and knowledge about the person and the environment compared to a system with no or insufficient data. Thus, there is a tricky trade-off between creating and providing smartness (by collecting and processing sufficiently many data for tailoring functionality to make the system 'smart') vs. providing or maintaining privacy, i.e. the right of people to be in control over which data are being collected, by whom and how they are processed and evaluated and to whom they are forwarded for further processing and storage. The challenge is now to find the right balance between the two objectives. It is proposed that determining the balance should be under the control of the respective person. This requires transparency about the options, which are not always provided by the different service providers to their users. The design trade-off between 'usable privacy vs. smartness' is illustrated in Fig. 3 below (taken from Streitz [39], where it is also discussed in more detail).

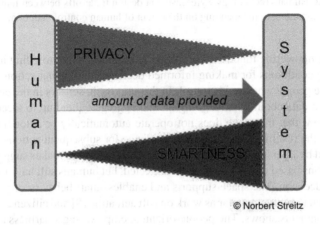

© Norbert Streitz

Fig. 3. Design trade-off between privacy by control over personal data vs. degree of smartness provided by a smart system or service.

The point to be stressed here is that this trade-off should be transparent and in control of the people who own the data in the first place. People often provide data for certain benefits (e.g., loyalty/ payback cards, lotteries, sweepstakes) and it seems to be a conscious decision. But one can argue if it is also an informed decision because many people are not aware of the real equivalent value of the data they provide. In this context, one must mention that there are also unnecessary trade-offs proposed. For example, why does a flash-light app on a smart phone require to have access to the list of phone calls and the address book with all contacts? These data are not necessary for providing the flash-light functionality. Unfortunately, trade-off procedures are in most cases neglected and people are not offered a choice. This is the reason why 'privacy by design' and 'privacy by default' must be adopted as guiding design principles and not to make it an add-on after the design and implementation process has been finalized. In other terms, one can also rephrase this goal orientation as 'from Big Data to Better Data' – better for the people by providing privacy and smartness, but under their control.

'Usable Privacy by Design and by Default' is now the challenge for system designers. They must be aware of it and must realize the trade-off options at the design as well as at the implementation stage. The result should enable and empower users so that they can make their personal, individual trade-off decisions in a transparent and usable way. Transparency means here that the users are informed about the implications of their decisions. Service providers and their system designers should be aware that this is – for already some time now – required by the European General Data Protection Regulations (EU-GDPR) [10], adopted already in 2016, which took effect on May 25, 2018. Furthermore, it should be possible for the users to have different settings for different applications and services. Their decisions should be revisable any time, and, very important, be respected by the system without questioning. These issues require a new way of thinking about the design of human-computer, resp. 'human-environment interaction' for making these choices transparent and easy to use. A similar approach needs to be formulated for 'Usable Security by Design and Default', but there is no space to address it in this paper here.

4.3 Ethical Design

The challenges created by the design trade-offs 'smartness vs. privacy' and 'human control vs. automation' are intricately related with ethical issues. Examples are obvious when thinking of automated driving, often called and considered as autonomous driving. Autonomous decision making and subsequent actions pose severe problems in life-critical situations, where the 'car' makes decisions, whether the passengers in the car or some pedestrians crossing the street must be killed (depending on certain parameters), because there is no other escape. This moral dilemma conflict is the updated version of the famous 'trolley problem' now applied to self-driving cars and was investigated at MIT (www.moralmachine.net) with surprising results showing quite some differences in people's attitudes. Therefore, it is no coincidence that the world's largest professional engineering community IEEE is engaged in the definition of a standards body on 'Ethically Aligned Design' (EAD) [9]. The efforts of the IEEE Global Initiative on Ethics of Autonomous and Intelligent Systems (A/IS) and its recommendations for ethically aligned design can be found at its website (https://ethicsinaction.ieee.org). Since there is no space here, I refer to a discussion of these recommendations by Streitz et al. [40].

5   From User-Centered Design to Citizen-Centered Design

The third focus of this paper addresses the transfer of the preceding argumentation lines and proposals to a specific and very relevant application domain: cities and their associated urban environments. The shift from human-computer interaction (HCI) towards human-environment interaction (HEI) is caused by the trend towards more comprehensive application contexts and urban environments. It requires a corresponding shift from a mostly individual person-based 'user'-centered design approach to a multiple people and multiple devices-based 'citizen-centered' design approach [35, 39]. But it is not only the multiple people and multiple devices aspect, it is also a shift in the needs and properties of the 'users'. This can be described as follows: 'humans' in the traditional 'human-computer-interaction' equation are not anymore only 'users' of 'computers', but rather 'citizens' inhabiting and appropriating urban environments (e.g., cities, airports), enhanced with smart technologies constituting smart ecosystems. This requires a very different design approach in meeting their needs. Thus, the shift from human-computer interaction (HCI) to human-environment interaction (HEI) must be further transformed to Citizen-Environment Interaction (CEI) [38] due to a new and comprehensive perspective needed in smart urban environments, also described by the hyped term 'smart city'. Citizens require participation in the design of their smart environments and want to contribute to it. In the next section of this paper, we will discuss how this shift plays a role when moving *beyond* 'smart-only' cities.

6 Beyond 'Smart-Only' Cities Towards Humane, Sociable and Cooperative Hybrid Cities

In the previous sections of this paper, the general issues of the 'smart-everything' paradigm and the general design trade-offs were discussed. Now, based on the shift from HCI to HEI and consequently CEI [38], it is time to apply these considerations to a concrete application domain by addressing the multiple problems that cities encounter in the urban age. Many people claim that the solution is provided by building 'smart cities', which became a world-wide hype fueled especially by large-scale industries and infrastructure companies. In the meantime, the term was associated with a multitude of meanings and connotations so that it turned into an empty buzzword. Many of these developments are unfortunately primarily technology driven. They do not account sufficiently for the role and rights of citizens as it is required from a citizen-centered design perspective that should be adopted in the large.

The proposal is therefore *to move beyond* 'smart-only' cities and to establish the goal of *Humane, Sociable and Cooperative Hybrid Cities* [35, 38, 39]. It is based on the efforts of redefining the 'smart-everything' paradigm and replacing a technology-driven notion of 'smart' by a citizen-oriented notion of 'cooperative'. The road towards this goal is provided by engaging in the design trade-offs as described in Sect. 4.1 on 'Human Control vs. Automated or Autonomous Systems' and in Sect. 4.2 'Smartness vs. Usable Privacy', guided by the overall design principle of human-technology symbiosis.

These design trade-offs have specific implications when applied to 'smart cities' and 'smart airports'. While privacy is already now an issue in the virtual world of social media and on-line communities, it will become even more relevant in the so-called 'smart cities' being proposed and developed. I prefer to speak here of '*hybrid cities*' [35, 37, 39], because we must consider an integrated design of real physical architectural spaces and virtual information spaces and models representing the digital, virtual world [30]. While in the virtual world, one can – to a certain degree – still use fake identities and anonymization services, it will be more difficult to achieve this kind of disguise in the real world. The data that exist about a person in the virtual world are now complemented by and combined with real world data and vice versa. Combined with the 'disappearing computer' property (discussed in Sect. 2), the large-scale challenge is how to provide information and affordances in future urban environments, so that people can discover easily what is going on. Even today and more so in the future, they are not fully aware of being tracked and monitored, because they cannot perceive the different sensors, the manifold smart devices embedded and distributed in the urban environment. The challenge is how to establish a 'calm technology' [53] and providing a citizen-oriented ambient intelligence, that supports and respects individual and social life by keeping the human in the loop and in control as well as the right of citizens in terms of privacy and security in a combined fashion.

6.1 Smart Cities as 'Self-Aware' Cities

The 'smartness of a city' can also be characterized by how much the city knows about itself and how this is communicated to the city administration and its citizens. This is the concept of the 'self-aware' city [37, 39]. There are two perspectives and advantages. First, city authorities in charge of administering and managing the city obtain additional knowledge about the different urban parameters and can take more informed decisions – in accordance with our earlier proposal (Sect. 4.1), that "smart spaces make people smarter". Second, citizens are enabled to have more comprehensive and augmented multiple views of their city. At the same time, it empowers them to engage and participate in addressing open city-related problems. In several cases, citizens will even play an active role in the data collection process. Examples are projects on 'open data' and civic apps [18]. A very active open data community can be found, for example, in Amsterdam.

Providing awareness and experiences are means to convey the status of the city. Examples are feedback on air and sound pollution levels in the city, congested traffic, numbers of bicycles used today and, in the past, (e.g., the 'Velo-Barometer' in the city of Luzern, Switzerland, provides this information in real-time in a public space), delayed buses and trains, broken roads, non-functioning devices, etc. Providing direct location-specific awareness, e.g., on pollution, by using an ambient display in a transient public space, can also be combined with an interactive art installation turning the city status communication into an enjoyable experience for the citizens. Other ways of communication are also useful: posting real time data on websites or via apps, providing personalized/ individualized awareness, using visual information via overlay displays (e.g., augmented reality type glasses), using local sound (in earphones) or tactile hints employing vibrations conveyed by your clothes using smart textiles. There is no general solution which must be used to convey the awareness information. The design decision depends on which human senses are appropriate and compatible for which situation.

Konomi et al. [17] developed a very good example of enabling and communicating this type of self-awareness by measuring urban congestion in trains of the Tokyo subway. It applies a clever approach of using indirect measures (the CO_2 level in the train compartments) for determining the congestion level (the more CO_2, the more passengers). This method is also an example that collecting necessary data involves active and consenting participation of citizens. Konomi [17] calls it the 'civic computing' approach, which is the perfect transition to the next section.

6.2 Goal-Orientation: What Kind of City Do We Want to Live in?

Obviously, all issues and design challenges mentioned before must be viewed in a coordinated and comprehensive perspective. One way to orient ourselves for establishing our design goals and objectives is to ask: What kind of future do we want? What kind of city do we want to live in? A technology-driven and importunate computer-, especially AI-dominated one? Probably not!

Answering these questions, requires formulating a different set of requirements and design goals in the first place guided by the principle of Human-Technology Symbiosis. I propose to use a rephrasing of 'smart' as "*smart, but only in the sense of being cooperative, sociable and humane*". In accordance with the design trade-offs and the ethical considerations presented in Sect. 4, the overall goal of designing and realizing future or refurbishing existing cities should be:

To build Humane, Sociable and Cooperative Hybrid Cities reconciling people and technology by providing a balance between human control and automation as well as privacy and smartness.

This implies to foster and enable the following seven actions and requirements (according to Streitz [39]):

- Establishing a calm technology providing ambient intelligence that supports and respects individual and social life by 'keeping the human in the loop and in control'.
- Respecting the rights of citizens, especially in terms of privacy and security. Therefore, personal data should – as much as possible – only be collected based on consent by providing choices and control of the process, including models of temporary provision and access and/or obligations to delete data later. EU-GDPR regulations provide a good basis to start with.
- Viewing the city and its citizens as mutual cooperation partners, where a city is 'smart' in the sense of being 'self-aware' and 'cooperative' towards its citizens by supporting them in their activities and making them smarter. This requires mutual trust and respect for the motives and vested interests of all stakeholders involved.
- Acknowledging the capabilities of citizens to participate in the design of the urban environment (=> participatory design), especially with respect to their local expertise, and stimulating their active participation and contributions.
- Motivating citizens to get involved, to understand themselves as part of the urban community, to be actively engaged by contributing to the public good and welfare (=> collective intelligence, mapping useful aspects found in the approach of the Greek 'agora' as a market-place of ideas).
- Enabling citizens to exploit their individual, creative, social, and economic potential and to live a self-determined life, and thus
- Meeting some of the challenges of the urban age by enabling people to experience and enjoy a satisfying life and work.

Figure 4 (taken from [39]) provides the global picture. It indicates the merging and integration of the real physical city with virtual representations of the city [30] into what is called a 'hybrid city' and its augmentation and provision with the characteristic features being the core of moving beyond the 'smart-only' city. The combined representations provide the basis for modeling the city and to define how the different parts can be augmented with smart properties and creating an urban environment with ambient intelligence features. One must determine how this augmentation can be used for the overall benefit of the city and providing added value for each individual citizen. This is the idea of moving beyond a 'smart-only' city and transforming the city into a 'smart, but cooperative, humane and sociable city'.

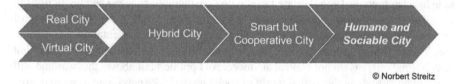

© Norbert Streitz

Fig. 4. Relationships and goal orientation of different city characteristics.

While the motivation for designing a 'humane city' [34, 35, 51] and a 'sociable city' [37] appears to be rather straight forward, the notion of a '*cooperative* city' might need some explanation. It is also based on our earlier work on 'cooperative buildings' and Roomware® [43, 44, 52]. In this tradition, it is proposed here to apply human-centered design principles that have proven useful, e.g., in human-computer interaction (HCI) and computer-supported cooperative work (CSCW), now in this context as Citizen-Centered Design. The 'cooperation' perspective is considered as an overarching goal for the design process. It allows integrating functionalities and policies from the very beginning, viewing citizens as prospective 'customers' of city services. This perspective results in what can be called 'city as a service', where the urban environment is the interface between the city and the citizens. A transparent urban ambient intelligence environment enables city authorities as well as citizens to make more and better-informed decisions, because *both* (and this is essential) parties can access and exploit the wealth of all the data collected. Still, one always should keep in mind, that 'smartness' is not a goal or value in itself. It must be evaluated against the needs of the citizens and the resulting design guidelines stated before. Therefore, a discussion in a cooperative and respectful manner is needed for contributing to the objectives of the *Cooperative Humane and Sociable City*.

7   Conclusions and Outlook

Having painted a somehow ideal and optimistic picture of what is or should be desirable, one has, of course, to be realistic and be aware that the 'smart' city, especially the 'smart-only' city, poses new challenges, because there are several potential pitfalls. One is the increasing commercialization of many aspects of urban life. It is no secret that the 'smart city' scenario is considered by many companies as the 'next big thing', where large profits are expected. If this trend continues and is dominated by a technology-driven perspective, it will result in fewer options for citizen participation in the decision-making process and more privacy infringements, because the commercial objectives will – in many cases – be different to those outlined above.

The British architect Cedric Price (1934–2003) expressed his concerns in the remark-able provocation '*Technology is the answer, but what was the question?*' which he used as the title of one of his lectures [25], inviting the audience to search, question, and reconsider the impact of technological progress on architecture. I think that the question is still relevant today and should be asked by every designer of smart environments especially now, because the impact of technology on us as humans and citizens and on society as a whole is much more dramatic compared with more than 50 years ago, when Price made his statement in 1966. We are faced with considerable changes and restrictions in the self-determination of our lives because we are losing control over the handling of our data. We are confronted with 'over-information' and 'under-orientation' at the same time. There is missing transparency and accountability of AI-based technologies, that we as normal citizens do not control anymore. As I pointed out above, this was and still is a problem already in the virtual world of social media, fake news, and to some degree on-line commerce, but now it will become even more relevant and dramatic in the real world of urban environments during their transformation to hybrid smart cities.

Thus, we must develop and foster approaches that reset the priorities and put humans in their different roles (as users and customers in particular and as citizens in general) first and computers and importunate AI-based automation technology second.

As an outlook for accomplishing a more humane and sociable 'cooperative city' environment [39], I propose for future work to define and establish first the framework and then the details of a *Citizen ⇔ Cooperative City Contract* (CCCC or C4). It will contain agreements between the involved stakeholders based on defined conditions and constraints. The agreements enable to negotiate the trade-offs on automation vs. control/empowerment and smartness vs. privacy. This requires open systems and software architectures and new approaches for the validation of negotiations, agreements, and contracts. Here, one could consider the proposal of so called 'smart contracts' based on block chain technology as an option for its realization. Appropriate interfaces for citizens as well as service providers are needed for the integration of their components overseeing the negotiations of the trade-offs. Participating stakeholders specify their requirements and parameters for an equitable negotiation and trade-off process for the benefit of all parties involved.

Despite all the unwanted developments and drawbacks on our way to maintain human control and empowerment as well as usable privacy as a first order design principle, we should keep the following in mind, because it also holds true in these times: we must expect everything - even the good!

References

1. Aarts, E., Encarnaçao, J. (eds.): True Visions. In: The emergence of ambient intelligence. Springer-Verlag (2006). https://doi.org/10.1007/978-3-540-28974-6
2. AI NOW: (2017). https://ainowinstitute.org/AI_Now_2017_Report.pdf
3. Angelidou, M.: The role of smart city characteristics in the plans of fifteen cities. Journal of Urban Technology 24(4), 3–28 (2017). https://doi.org/10.1080/10630732.2017.1348880
4. Baecker, R., Buxton, W. (eds.): Readings in Human-Computer Interaction. Morgan Kaufmann, Burlington (1987)
5. Card, S., Moran, T., Newell, A.: The Psychology of Human-Computer Interaction. Lawrence Erlbaum Ass, Mahwah (1983)
6. Crevier, D.: AI: The Tumultuous Search for Artificial Intelligence. Basic Books, New York (1993)
7. Crowley, D.N., Curry, E., Breslin, J.G.: Citizen actuation for smart environments. IEEE Consumer Electronics Magazine 5(3), 90–94 (2016)

8. Domaszewicz, J., Lalis, S., Pruszkowski, A., Koutsoubelias, M., Tajmajer, T., Grigoropoulos, N.: Soft actuation: smart home and office with human-in-the-loop. IEEE Pervasive Computing **15**(1), 48–56 (2016)

9. EAD – Ethically Aligned Design, version 2. https://ethicsinaction.ieee.org/

10. EU-GDPR: (2016). http://www.eugdpr.org/ and more specific http://www.privacy-regulation. eu/en/13.htm and https://www.privacy-regulation.eu/en/22.htm

11. Gibson, J.J.: The Senses Considered as Perceptual Systems. Allen and Unwin, Crows Nest (1966)

12. Gibson, J.J.: The Ecological Approach to Visual Perception. Houghton Mifflin Harcourt, Boston (1979)

13. Greif, I.: Computer-Supported Cooperative Work: A Book of Readings. Morgan Kaufmann Publishers, Burlington (1988)

14. Hoschka, P., Butscher, B., Streitz, N.: Telecooperation and telepresence: technical challenges of a government distributed between Bonn and Berlin. Informatization and the public sector **2**(4), 269–299 (1993)

15. ISTAG: Scenarios for Ambient Intelligence in 2010. Final report. European Commission, Luxembourg, February 2001

16. Johannsen, A., Haake, J.M., Streitz, N.A.: Telekooperation in Virtuellen Organisationen: Potentiale verteilter Sitzungsunterstützungssysteme. Wirtschaftsinformatik. **40**(3), 214–222 (1998)

17. Konomi, S., Shoji, K., Ohno, W.: Rapid Development of Civic Computing Services: Opportunities and Challenges. In: Streitz, N., Stephanidis, C. (eds.) DAPI 2013. LNCS, vol. 8028, pp. 309–315. Springer, Heidelberg (2013). https://doi.org/10.1007/978-3-642-39351-8_34

18. Lee, M., Almirall, E., Wareham, J.: Open data and civic apps: first-generation failures, second-generation improvements. Communications of the ACM **59**(1), 82–89 (2016)

19. Magerkurth, C., Stenzel, R., Streitz, N., Neuhold, E.: A multimodal interaction framework for pervasive game applications. In: Workshop at Artificial Intelligence in Mobile System (AIMS 2003), 12 October 2003, Seattle, USA, pp. 1–8 (2003)

20. Mark, G., Haake, J.M., Streitz, N.A.: Hypermedia structures and the division of labor in meeting room collaboration. In: Proceedings of ACM Conference CSCW 1996, Boston, 16–20 November 1996, pp. 170–179 (1996)

21. Norman, D.A.: The Psychology of Everyday Things (POET). Basic Books, New York (1988). (revised version published as The Design of Everyday Things.)

22. Norman, D.A.: Affordance, conventions and design. Interactions **6**(3), 38–43 (1999). ACM Press

23. Norman, D.A., Draper, S.: User Centered System Design: New Perspectives on Human-Computer Interaction. Lawrence Erlbaum Associates, Mahwah (1986)

24. Prante, T., Stenzel, R., Röcker, C., Streitz, N., Magerkurth, C.: Ambient Agoras: InfoRiver, Siam, Hello. Wall. In: CHI 2004 Extended Abstracts of ACM Conference on Human Factors in Computing Systems, 24–29 April 2004, Vienna, Austria, pp. 763–764 (2004)

25. Price, C.: Technology is the answer, but what was the question? Title of Lecture (1966)

26. Russell, D., Streitz, N., Winograd, T.: Building disappearing computers. Communications of the ACM **48**(3), 42–48 (2005)

27. Stephanidis, C., et al.: Seven HCI grand challenges. International Journal of Human-Computer Interaction **35**(14), 1229–1269 (2019). https://doi.org/10.1080/10447318.2019. 1619259

28. Streitz, N.: Cognitive ergonomics: an approach for the design of user oriented interactive systems. In: Klix, F., Wandke, H. (eds.), Man-Computer Interaction Research - MACINTER-I. North-Holland Publisher, pp. 21–33 (1986)

29. Streitz, N.: Cognitive compatibility as a central issue in human-computer interaction: theoretical framework and empirical findings. In: Salvendy, G. (ed.) Cognitive Engineering in the Design of Human-Computer Interaction and Expert Systems. Elsevier Science Publishers, pp. 75–82 (1987)

30. Streitz, N.A.: Integrated design of real architectural spaces and virtual information spaces. In: CHI 1998 Conference Summary on Human Factors in Computing Systems, pp. 263–264, April 1998

31. Streitz, N.: Augmented Reality and the Disappearing Computer. In: Smith, M., Salvendy, G., Harris, D., Koubek, R. (eds.) Cognitive Engineering, Intelligent Agents and Virtual Reality, pp. 738–742. Lawrence Erlbaum, Mahwah (2001)

32. Streitz, N.A.: From Human–Computer Interaction to Human–Environment Interaction: Ambient Intelligence and the Disappearing Computer. In: Stephanidis, C., Pieper, M. (eds.) UI4ALL 2006. LNCS, vol. 4397, pp. 3–13. Springer, Heidelberg (2007). https://doi.org/10.1007/978-3-540-71025-7_1

33. Streitz, N.: The disappearing computer. In: Erickson, T., McDonald, D.W. (eds.) HCI Remixed: Reflections on Works that have Influenced the HCI Community. MIT Press, pp. 55–60 (2008)

34. Streitz, N.A.: Smart cities, ambient intelligence and universal access. In: Stephanidis, C. (ed.) UAHCI 2011. LNCS, vol. 6767, pp. 425–432. Springer, Heidelberg (2011). https://doi.org/10.1007/978-3-642-21666-4_47

35. Streitz, N.: Citizen-centered design for humane and sociable hybrid cities. In: Theona, I., Charitos, D. (eds.) Hybrid City 2015 - Data to the People. Proceedings of the Third International Biannual Conference. University of Athens, Greece, pp. 17–20 (2015)

36. Streitz, N.: Smart Cities need privacy by design for being humane. In: Pop, S., Toft, T., Calvillo, N., Wright, M. (eds.), What Urban Media Art Can Do - Why When Where and How? Avedition, pp. 268–274 (2016)

37. Streitz, N.: Reconciling humans and technology: the role of ambient intelligence. In: Braun, A., Wichert, R., Maña, A. (eds.) AmI 2017. LNCS, vol. 10217, pp. 1–16. Springer, Cham (2017). https://doi.org/10.1007/978-3-319-56997-0_1

38. Streitz, N.: The Future of human-computer interaction: from HCI to citizen-environment interaction (CEI) in cooperative cities and societies. In: Proceedings of the 2nd International Conference on Computer-Human Interaction Research and Applications (CHIRA 2018), SCITEPRESS, pp. 7–13 (2018). ISBN: 978-989-758-328-5

39. Streitz, N.: Beyond 'smart-only' cities: redefining the 'smart-everything' paradigm. Journal of Ambient Intelligence and Humanized Computing 10(2), 791–812 (2019). https://doi.org/10.1007/s12652-018-0824-1

40. Streitz, N., Charitos, D., Kaptein, M., Böhlen, M.: Grand challenges for ambient intelligence and implications for design contexts and smart societies. Journal of Ambient Intelligence and Smart Environments 11(1), 87–107. (IOS Press) (2019). https://doi.org/10.3233/ais-180507

41. Streitz, N., et al.: SEPIA: a cooperative hypermedia authoring environment. In: Proceedings of ACM European Conference on Hypertext (ECHT 1992), pp. 11–22 (1992)

42. Streitz, N., Geißler, J., Haake, J., Hol, J.: DOLPHIN: integrated meeting support across local and remote desktop environments and LiveBoards. In: Proceedings of the 1994 ACM Conference on Computer Supported Cooperative Work (CSCW 1994), pp. 345–358 (1994)

43. Streitz, N.A., Geißler, J., Holmer, T.: Roomware for cooperative buildings: integrated design of architectural spaces and information spaces. In: Streitz, N.A., Konomi, S., Burkhardt, H.-J. (eds.) CoBuild 1998. LNCS, vol. 1370, pp. 4–21. Springer, Heidelberg (1998). https://doi.org/10.1007/3-540-69706-3_3

44. Streitz, N., et al.: i-LAND: an interactive landscape for creativity and innovation. In: Proceedings of ACM CHI 1999 Conference on Human Factors in Computing Systems, pp. 120–127. ACM Press (1999)

45. Streitz, N., Kameas, A., Mavrommati, I. (eds.): The Disappearing Computer. LNCS, vol. 4500. Springer, Heidelberg (2007). https://doi.org/10.1007/978-3-540-72727-9

46. Streitz, N., Nixon, P.: The disappearing computer. Guest editors' introduction to special issue. Communications of the ACM **48**, 33–35 (2005)

47. Streitz, N., et al.: Smart artefacts as affordances for awareness in distributed teams. In: Streitz, N., Kameas, A., Mavrommati, I. (eds.) The Disappearing Computer. LNCS, vol. 4500, pp. 3–29. Springer, Heidelberg (2007). https://doi.org/10.1007/978-3-540-72727-9_1

48. Streitz, N., Privat, G.: Ambient intelligence. Final section 'Looking to the Future'. In: Stephanidis, C. (ed.) The Universal Access Handbook, pp. 60.1–60.17. CRC Press (2009)

49. Streitz, N., Rexroth, P., Holmer, T.: Anforderungen an interaktive Kooperationslandschaften für kreatives Arbeiten und erste Realisierungen. In: Herrmann, T., Just-Hahn, K. (eds.), Groupware und organisatorische Innovation – Proceedings of D-CSCW 1998. Stuttgart. Teubner-Verlag, pp. 237–250 (1998)

50. Streitz, N., Röcker, C., Prante, T., van Alphen, D., Stenzel, R., Magerkurth, C.: Designing Smart Artifacts for Smart Environments. IEEE Computer **38**(3), 41–49 (2005). https://doi.org/10.1109/MC.2005.92

51. Streitz, N., Wichert, R.: Towards the humane city: white paper on a future research agenda for ambient computing. Report of the EU-funded project InterLink, pp. 15–24 (2009). https://www.ercim.eu/publication/policy/interlink-booklet-opt.pdf

52. Tandler, P., Streitz, N., Prante, T.: Roomware - moving toward ubiquitous computers. IEEE Micro **22**(6), 36–47 (2002)

53. Weiser, M.: The computer for the 21st century. Scientific American **265**(3), 66–75 (1991)

Computer-Human Interaction in Music Composition Through Petri Nets

Adriano Baratè⊚, Goffredo Haus⊚, and Luca Andrea Ludovico^(✉)⊚

Laboratorio di Informatica Musicale (LIM), Dipartimento di Informatica "Giovanni
Degli Antoni", Università degli Studi di Milano,
Via Giovanni Celoria 18, 20133 Milan, Italy
{adriano.barate,goffredo.haus,luca.ludovico}@unimi.it

Abstract. Petri nets are a well-known mathematical formalism usually applied to the fields of information representation and manipulation. Scientific literature has demonstrated their applicability to the field of music analysis, thanks to the possibility to achieve a clear description of music processes and transformations, to obtain easy-to-understand graphical representation, and to use formal tools for net analysis. More remarkably, the adoption of Petri nets can foster also music creation, above all for compositions based on the transformation of music objects. Nevertheless, there is a gap between the way a music piece is typically conceived and the way it can be described in terms of Petri nets, or another equivalent formal tools. The goal of the present work is to demonstrate how digital approaches rooted in computer-human interaction can bridge such a gap, thus fostering both creativity and analytical activities in music composition processes.

Keywords: Music · Composition · Computer-human interaction · Petri nets · Web editor

1 Introduction

Music in the last centuries has evolved from many perspectives: musical instruments' features [41], composing and performing techniques [31], new kinds of notation [20], new distribution forms [25], etc. Just like mechanical reproducibility had a deep impact on music experience, the recent advent of digital tools and methodologies have transformed traditional aesthetic definitions [16].

Within a wide range of aspects of potential interest, we will focus on music-composition processes and their evolution in the digital era. The goal of this paper is to highlight the importance of computer-based tools suitable to unleash creativity by supporting heterogeneous composing techniques, ranging from common notation to the manipulation of audio fragments. In this sense, music, musicology, computer science, digital technology, mathematical formalism, etc. would not be sufficient in themselves; rather, a multidisciplinary approach is necessary. This need is clearly pointed out by recent file formats for score representation;

© Springer Nature Switzerland AG 2021
M. J. Escalona et al. (Eds.): CHIRA 2018/CHIRA 2019, CCIS 1351, pp. 60–79, 2021.
https://doi.org/10.1007/978-3-030-67108-2_4

even if symbolic aspects (i.e. traditional notation) are still central, relevant initiatives such as IEEE 1599 [2], MEI [40], and MusicXML [19] support also graphical, audio, video, textual, and even structural information, thus implementing the concept of *multi-layer description* of music [8].

A way to organize heterogeneous information and make composition processes explicit is to adopt a mathematical formalism in order to describe both music objects and their transformations. In this work, the chosen formalism is the one of Petri nets, already investigated in scientific literature as a valid means to represent concurrent processes; nevertheless, the same approach could be followed with other formal description tools. The research question we address is how to match the potentialities of a mathematical formalism with the way of conceiving a music work typical of a 21st Century composer. As explained below, our belief is that an answer can be found in the field of computer-human interaction, thanks to the design and implementation of suitable software tools acting as both editors and players. This paper is an extension of the work presented at the 2nd International Conference on Computer-Human Interaction Research and Applications (CHIRA), held in Sevilla, Spain in 2018 [7]. In that occasion, we presented a theoretical framework to compose music with Petri nets, supporting basically three types of music objects: symbolic objects, computer-driven performance objects, and audio objects. In the light of some additional work occurred in the last months, we achieved two key developments:

1. The implementation of a Web editor for music Petri nets, somehow different from the sketch presented in [7];
2. An extension of the original theoretical framework, mainly due to the awareness that a clear distinction between notation, computer-driven performance and audio could be of little worth in contemporary music.

The rest of the paper is structured as follows: Sect. 2 will present some noticeable experiences of computer interfaces supporting music composition, Sect. 3 will provide the key concepts about Petri nets and some noticeable extensions, Sect. 4 will discuss the applicability of Petri nets to the music field, Sect. 5 will focus on the potentialities and challenges posed by Petri nets in music composition, Sect. 6 will demonstrate the importance of computer-human interaction in order to respond to the composer's needs, and finally Sect. 7 will draw conclusions.

2   Related Work

Finding suitable interfaces to represent and manipulate music information is a relevant research question in the field of sound and music computing. In this sense, it is worth citing an early work by Joel Chadabe focusing on music composition and performance through computer systems, where the music creation process was organised into two steps: 1. the design of a compositional process, and 2. the interaction with the machine playback of that process when provided with suitable inputs. In 1985, an inspiring survey on computer-music interfaces and their basic principles was published [34], focusing on three musical tasks: manuscript preparation, music language interfaces for composition, and real-time performance interaction.

In more recent years, more and more computer-based instruments have been designed to help musicians, also as a consequence of the spread of electronic music elements and an increasingly blurred distinction between the composer and the performer.

As a noticeable example, IRCAM – a French institute for science about sound and music with a long tradition in the field of computer-assisted composition [1] – has developed and released *OpenMusic* (OM), a visual programming language for computer-assisted music composition based on Common Lisp [10]. Programs are created by assembling and connecting icons representing functions and data structures. From its first release in the late 90s, the ongoing development activity led to the creation of a high number of extensions, thus supporting various kinds of compositional approaches, based on aleatoric processes, constraint programming [45], sound spatialization [18], artificial intelligence and machine learning [46], and others.

MAX/Msp [48] and Pure Data [38] are dataflow programming languages where functions or objects are linked in a graphical environment which models control and audio flows. These software tools can also support formal approaches to composition and manipulation of music information, an aspect that brings them closer to our proposal. While OpenMusic is more oriented towards compositional/analysis tasks, MAX/Msp and Pure Data are often used in real time to manipulate sounds and create interactive performances.

A recent work [17], similar to the approach presented below, describes a framework designed to represent musical structures as simple sequences of timed components, called *timed items*, that can be used both to specify the inner structure of musical objects, and to organize them within compound structures.

The subject of computer-based tools and interfaces to support music composition could embrace many other aspects, such as design principles for computer music controllers and trends in electronic music interfaces ([12,33,44], to cite but a few). Besides, it would be worth mentioning many other works about this subject presented at annual conferences dedicated to sound and music computing, such as the International Conference on New Interfaces for Musical Expression (NIME), the Sound and Music Computing conference (SMC), the International Conference on Technologies for Music Notation and Representation (TENOR); unfortunately, for the sake of brevity we have to limit our review to composition-oriented frameworks.

3   Petri Nets Fundamentals

A Petri net (PN) is a formal tool that can help studying and describing concurrent, asynchronous, distributed, parallel, and non-deterministic systems [36]. A PN can be seen as an abstract formal model to represent the dynamic behavior of a system with asynchronous and concurrent activities.

The success of PNs is also due to simplicity. A PN is a combination of objects belonging to one of three categories: *places*, *transitions*, and *arcs*. Places and transitions are also referred to as *nodes*. Places can be connected to transitions only, and transitions to places only; this connection role is played by arcs. Arcs can have a number associated, called the *arc weight*.

PNs are used to track the evolution of a system from a state to another. The current state is indicated by the *place marking*, represented by the number of tokens in each place. Another key property of places is their capacity, namely the maximum number of tokens that the place can contain.

The dynamic evolution of a PN is determined by the following *firing rules*:

- A transition is enabled when all the incoming places of that transition present a number of tokens greater or equal to the weights of the corresponding incoming arcs, and, after the fire of the transition, the marking of all the output places will be less than or equal to their capacities;
- When a transition is enabled, its firing subtracts from the incoming places a number of tokens equal to the weights of the incoming arcs, and adds to each outgoing place a number of tokens equal to the weights of the corresponding outgoing arc.

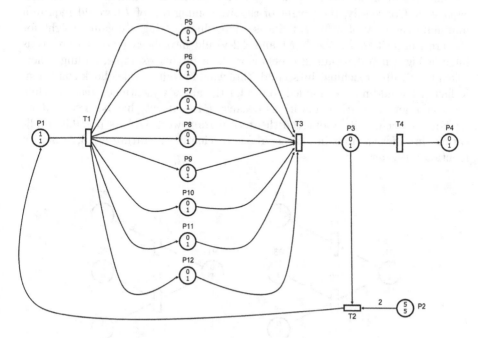

Fig. 1. An example of Petri net containing 12 places and 4 transitions.

Formally, a PN structure is a directed weighted bipartite graph

$$N = (P, T, A, w)$$

where P is the finite set of places ($P \neq \emptyset$), T is the finite set of transitions ($T \neq \emptyset$), $A = (P \times T) \cup (T \times P)$ is the set of arcs from places to transitions and from transitions to places, and $w : A \rightarrow \{1, 2, 3, \dots\}$ is the weight function on the arcs.

PNs are typically represented in a graphical way, where places are drawn as circles, transitions as rectangles, and arcs as oriented lines. Arc weights, place markings and place capacities are usually represented in numeric form. Figure 1 shows an example where all places are labeled as Px, all transitions as Ty, upper numbers in places represent the marking (i.e. the current number of tokens), lower numbers represent the capacity (i.e. the maximum number of tokens allowed), and numbers over arcs are present only if the arc weight is not the default one, namely 1.

An example that shows the marking of a net before and after a firing event is provided in Fig. 2. In this case, the only transition enabled to fire is $T2$, since all the incoming places ($P1$) present a number of tokens greater or equal to the weights of the corresponding incoming arcs, and, after the fire of the transition, the marking of all the output places ($P3$ and $P4$) are less than or equal to their capacities. Conversely, the weight of the arc coming out of $T1$ would require a minimum capacity of 3 for $P2$. Please note that, setting a default weight for the arc from $T1$ to $P2$, both $T1$ and $T2$ would have been ready to fire, thus introducing a non-deterministic behavior. As a further example, adding a new token to $P1$ after reaching the second state would produce a deadlock condition: in fact, $T1$ would not be enabled to fire for the already mentioned reason, while $T2$ would not meet firing conditions because $P4$'s capacity has been saturated.

For further details about the theoretical framework and its possible applications in different domains, please refer to scientific literature – [13,24,35], to mention but a few.

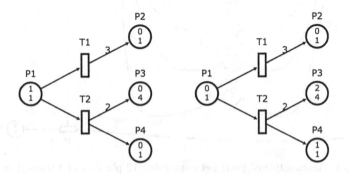

Fig. 2. States of a net before (left) and after (right) the firing of transition $T2$: 1 token in $P1$ is consumed, while 2 tokens and 1 token are deposited into $P3$ and $P4$ respectively.

Some extensions to the original theoretical framework are particularly relevant in the domain of this paper. The first extension is *refinement*, a simple morphism used to describe complex PNs in terms of simpler ones, in a hierarchical way. A refinement, called *subnet*, represents an entire PN that replaces a node; the subnet must have both an input and an output node of the same type of the refined node. The concept of hierarchical decomposition of a net has been explored in [27]. The importance of such an approach in the music domain is, on one side, the possibility to describe a piece at different levels of abstraction and aggregation, and, on the other side, the identification of recurrent structures as subnets to be re-used.

A second extension is *temporization*. Pure PNs do not implement the concept of time, so there are no strict temporal constraints in the evolution of a net. For example, the original theory does not force a transition to fire as soon as it is enabled to, and there is no duration associated to states (the time spent without changes in marking) and transitions (the time required to switch from a state to another). But, as specified in Sect. 4, music processes are temporized and music objects present a temporal dimension, thus time has to be introduced in the theoretical framework. Such an extension is known in scientific literature as *timed Petri nets*, and has been studied since the early days [39]. In timed PNs, the transitions fire in real-time, i.e., there is a firing time associated with each transition, the tokens are removed from input places at the beginning of firing, and are deposited into output places when the firing terminates [49]. A discussion about the theory and applications of timed PNs can be found in [47].

The last extension is the introduction of *probabilistic weight* for arcs, that is a way to solve conflicts and deal with non-determinism. Thanks to this feature, when many transitions are enabled, the choice depends on the probabilistic weight of the arcs involved, in relation with the total sum of their weights. The example in Fig. 3 reworks the one presented in Fig. 2 by changing arc weights and introducing probabilistic weights, represented inside square brackets. In this case, the non-determinism is solved by giving a non-zero weight to $T1$ only: the meaning is that, as long as $T1$ is enabled to fire, it will always fire, thus disabling the other transition; $T2$ will fire only if there are no other alternative or conflicting arcs with greater probabilistic weight, which never happens in the example provided. By changing weights (e.g., setting them to [10] and [10]), it is possible to introduce probabilistic behaviors (e.g., making either $T1$ or $T2$ fire with equal probability). The theme of probability in PNs has been explored in many scientific works, including [26,30] and [32].

The importance of PN extensions in the music domain will be discussed in Sect. 4.1.

4   Petri Nets in Music

PNs have been originally conceived to describe information-related processes. Their applicability to the music domain in order to investigate musical processes has been explored since the early '90s at the Laboratorio di Informatica Musicale

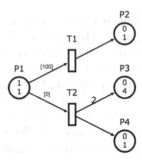

Fig. 3. A net with probabilistic arc weights in square brackets.

(LIM),[1] a research center on sound and music computing of the Department of Computer Science, University of Milan.

The considerations that guided pioneering research in this field were the support offered by PNs to hierarchical descriptions, the possibility to define multi-layer aggregations and macro-structures, the intrinsic ability to track the processing and transformations of music objects, the availability of a simple and easy-to-understand form of notation. In this context, PNs demonstrated to be suitable for the representation and processing of music objects and for the description of deterministic as well as non-deterministic models [22].

Early research resulted in the formalization of Music Petri nets (MPNs), a specialized extension of PNs that supports the association of music objects to places. A music object (MO) may be any information entity that carries a musical meaning, either simple or complex, either abstract or very detailed. MOs can be combined, reused as they are, or transformed into new ones. Different types of music-related content can be associated with places:

- *Symbolic content* – The MO contains score excerpts encoded in terms of Common Western Notation (e.g., notes, rests, etc.) or other notation systems;
- *Performance content* – The MO embeds information encoded through a computer-driven performance language, such as MIDI or SASL/SAOL;
- *Audio content* – The MO contains waveforms.

At present, this rigid distinction formalized in early research should be relaxed, since there are formal tools, technologies and formats for computer-aided composition that overcome it. For example, a Csound orchestra+score file potentially contains symbolic, performance and audio content, represents a computer-driven performance in itself, and produces audio content; similar considerations can be done for a MAX/Msp or a Pure Data patch.

In MPNs, since places can host MOs, transitions allow their transformation in order to produce new MOs. When working on symbolic content, manipulation typically involves music parameters such as pitch and duration; thus, it is possible to associate algorithms such as "transpose all notes of the first measure one

---

[1] https://www.lim.di.unimi.it.

octave below", or "double the duration of all C-pitched notes". On the opposite side, dealing with audio content, a transition can modify sound parameters, e.g., introducing volume changes, variations in equalization, pitch shifting, time stretching, etc.

For the sake of clarity, in MPNs places are not strictly required to host a MO. The net can still employ places with their traditional roles, such as counters, switches, and so on. In detail, a place:

- can host a MO that will be transferred to output places after the firing of the corresponding transitions. In this case, the fragment will be delivered to output places after the manipulation operated by transitions;
- can receive a MO from either a single or multiple input transitions. If multiple MOs arrive simultaneously and/or a MO is already present, they are mixed to form a more complex MO, potentially available for outgoing transitions;
- can have no MO in input and no MO associated. In this case, the place has only a structural function (e.g., a counter, a selector, a semaphore, etc.) in a given net topology, in accordance with the definition of places in traditional PNs, where marking represents the state of the system.

Moreover, in MPNs a place can be either enabled to play MOs or not. When an enabled place containing a MO receives tokens, the fragment (either already present or transferred from other places) is played; when a non-enabled place hosts or receives MOs, its only role is to mix inputs, store fragments and send them in output when transitions fire. The latter operation can be not trivial, above all when MO types to be mixed are heterogeneous.

Concerning transitions, in MPNs they can host algorithms to process MOs in input, modify them accordingly, and transfer the obtained MOs in output. A clarifying example, focusing on symbolic content, will be presented in Sect. 4.2, after recalling the role of the extensions introduced in Sect. 3.

4.1 The Role of PN Extensions

With respect to the original net theory, we have introduced 3 extensions: refinement, temporization, and probabilistic weight.

The importance of *refinement* in MPNs is the possibility to describe a music composition at various levels of abstraction, thanks to the introduction of subnets. This is not only a way to make the visual representation more compact, and, consequently, clearer to read, but also a means to catch two typical properties of a music composition: 1. its hierarchical structure, made of several levels with different degrees of abstraction; 2. the re-use of some materials, once again at different degrees of abstraction.

Concerning the former issue, recent theories show that music is intrinsically hierarchical, and the process of decomposition of music objects into simpler ones can occur recursively, until the most atomic level (e.g., the one of music symbols) has been reached [28]. Recent studies in the field of music theory, music cognition, and computational musicology has brought to the formulation of a generative theory where musical processes are made explicit, so as to unveil the structure of individual compositions [29].

With respect to the latter issue, namely the re-use of MOs, their very broad definition in terms of any meaningful aggregation of symbols, at different degrees of abstraction, comes in handy. Examples of music objects may be sections, periods, phrases, motifs, chord sequences, rhythmic patterns, etc. For the sake of clarity, let us consider a typical song structure in modern popular music: (intro), verse, pre-chorus, chorus (or refrain), verse, pre-chorus, chorus, bridge, verse, chorus and outro. Each part can be described through a subnet, and the subnets for verse, pre-chorus and chorus can be re-used, without redefining them from scratch. Other examples are particularly relevant in some classical music forms, such as the canon (a melody and its imitations) and the fugue (subject – answer – countersubject).

Another extension, namely temporization, is strictly required since MOs present a time dimension (e.g., note durations), and their performance must occur at a predictable timing. Moreover, the production of new MOs achieved by MPN transitions must be instantaneous, as well as the mixing and performing operations delegated to MPN places.

Finally, the extension of probabilistic weight lets us take into account all those non-deterministic forms of composition, particularly relevant in the experimentation of the last century [4, 11, 37], but already investigated in the past [23].

4.2 Example

In this section, we briefly present an example that transforms an input MO carrying symbolic content into a more complex aggregation of MOs.

Let us consider a net where place $P1$ is connected to place $P2$ through transition $T1$, and $P2$ to $P3$ through transitions $T2$ and $T3$ (Fig. 4). Moreover, places $P4$ and $P5$ are attached to transitions $T2$ and $T3$ respectively, and their role will be clarified soon. $P1$ hosts a MO, but its *Play* flag is set to false, so it does not perform it. $T1$ makes a copy of the MO, and puts both MOs in $P2$. Also $P2$ has the *Play* flag set to false. Now the two MOs could be distributed among $T2$ and $T3$, or both passed to either $T2$ or $T3$. The function of places $P4$ and $P5$, that do not host any MO, is to enable the single firing of both $T2$ and $T3$; in this way, the MOs contained in $P2$ are routed on two different paths. $T2$ consumes one of the MOs in $P2$, transposes it one major third above, then replicates it one grade up for other 3 times, following the schema of a major scale built on the first note of the original fragment. In the repetitions, rhythmic figures are maintained. $T3$ consumes the other MO in $P2$, extracts the duration of the first note (if any), extends it to the duration of the whole MO and multiplies it by 4, thus producing a pedal note. Finally, $P3$ mixes the MOs coming from $T2$ and $T3$ and plays them together. Figure 5 shows the result when the MO in $P1$ is a single D-pitched note (left) and when the MO is a sequence of notes (right).

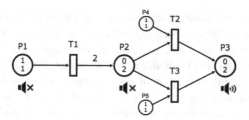

Fig. 4. A net that duplicates, manipulates, mixes and performs the original MO in input.

Fig. 5. Results obtained by the net in Fig. 4 when the MO is a single note (left) or a note sequence (right).

5   Composing Music with Petri Nets

Adopting the generative theory mentioned above, complex musical compositions can be considered as the result of transformational processes at different degrees of abstraction. Parts and voices can be seen as parallel, concurrent and distributed sequences of MOs, which, in turn, can be decomposed into simpler information entities.

In this context, the first research question emerging from the application of PNs to music composition is: Can repertoire pieces be easily and effectively described in terms of MPNs? Previous research and scientific literature provide some answers. Works such as [5] and [21], where MPNs have been applied to the formalization of the 1st movement of Mozart's *Piano Sonata KV 332* and Ravel's *Bolero* respectively, seem to suggest an affirmative answer. Conversely, the same approach applied to the formalization of Stravinskij's *The Rite of Spring* highlights a number of issues [14]. However, there is no contradiction between these results, since the success of the formalization task largely depends on two factors:

1. The level of granularity to reach – When addressing high-level musical structures, MPNs have proved to be a valid tool; when aiming to describe single score symbols, conversely, they show a number of limits;
2. The composition style, genre and form – For those methods of composition based on recognizable sequences of pitches, rhythms, or other musical elements, such as counterpoint or serialism, it is easier to describe a music piece in terms of MPNs, also reaching a fine level of granularity.

In this context, we are more interested in the possible application of MPNs to composition than in analysis of already-existing pieces. Some efforts in this direction are already available in literature. For example, Baratè et al. [9] propose a formalization of Schoenberg's fundamentals in terms of MPNs, starting from two didactic works authored by the renowned composer [42,43]. However, the mentioned approach was basically a way to investigate if MPN theory could be applied to traditional principles of composition, so as to improve the comprehension of the underlying musical processes; in this sense, the adoption of a mathematical formalism offers the possibility to support and – in some cases – even automatize analytical processes. However, this a-posteriori activity that does not present a real advancement in terms of musical expression.

An interesting application of MPNs for music composition, supporting real-time changes in marking and even in net topology during its evolution, is discussed in [6].

6   The Role of Computer-Human Interaction

The success of a format, a standard, a formalism does not depend only on its efficacy or potential, but also on its usability and, ultimately, on the wide adoption by final users. In this sense, the role of computer-human interaction clearly emerges. MPNs have been explored in scientific literature and their efficacy in describing music processes (at least at a high level of abstraction) has been demonstrated, but, as far as we know, they have never been adopted as a composition tool.

The research team on MPNs at the University of Milan organized some focus groups involving musicians interested in computer-aided composition and formal authoring tools. On the one hand, a great curiosity towards MPNs emerged, but, on the other, the lack of ad-hoc software tools to plan, refine and test such nets was recognized as a critical issue. Test users were able to understand the expressive power of MPNs, but they did non feel comfortable with such a formalism, rather suggesting a programming-block approach. These observations pushed us to design user-friendly editors for MPNs.

Currently, a number of software tools for the design and execution of generic PNs is available. PIPE (Platform Independent Petri net Editor)[2] is an open-source, platform-independent application for creating and analysing PNs, including Generalised Stochastic PNs [15]. The Petri Net Toolbox[3] is a software tool for the simulation, analysis, and design of discrete-event systems based on Petri Net models embedded in the MATLAB environment. WoPeD (Workflow Petri Net Designer)[4] is an open-source software which aims to provide an easy-to-use interface for modelling, simulating and analyzing processes described by workflow nets.

---

[2] http://pipe2.sourceforge.net/.

[3] https://www.mathworks.com/products/connections/product_detail/petri-net-tool box.html.

[4] https://woped.dhbw-karlsruhe.de/.

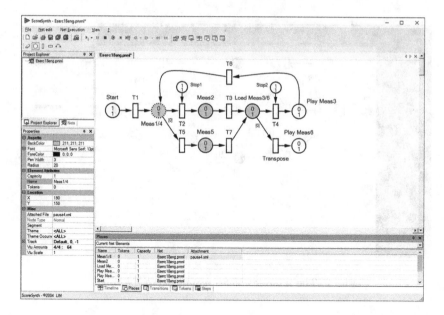

Fig. 6. The interface of *ScoreSynth* for Microsoft Windows.

6.1 ScoreSynth

Concerning MPNs, the only tool available so far was *ScoreSynth*, first released
in the early '90s [22], and then reprogrammed in C# to run under later versions
of Microsoft Windows; recent tests have demonstrated also a good compatibility
with Linux-based operating systems, thanks to the Mono project.[5] The main goal
of *ScoreSynth* is to draw and execute MPNs supporting MOs encoded in IEEE
1599 format [3]. Multiple windows permit to arrange all Petri nets that con-
cur to design a single complex model. Customizable graphical elements include:
place and transition sizes; place and transition names with user-defined positions;
place, transition, and arc background and foreground colors; arc smoothness; pen
widths; fonts; drawing grids. The interface of *ScoreSynth* is shown in Fig. 6.

In *ScoreSynth*, MPNs can be executed and debugged in three ways:

1. Complete execution – The standard execution mode, where nets are processed
   until no transition can fire, or the user stops the execution;
2. Timed execution – Similar to the complete execution, but transition firings
   occurs every n seconds;
3. Step-by-step execution – The user controls the process by triggering single
   steps, such as transition firings, tokens transfer, performance of MOs.

To ease debugging operations, an automatic step-by-step text report of net
execution is provided. The execution history is saved too, and the user can invoke

---

[5] https://www.mono-project.com/.

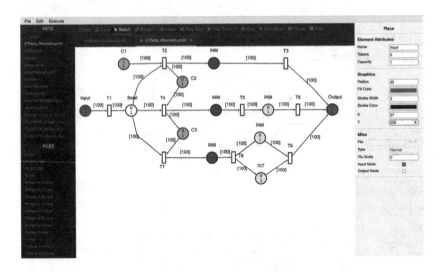

Fig. 7. The interface of *ScoreSynth Web Edition*.

previous-step and next-step buttons. In addition to exploring the execution history, this function is also useful to test non-deterministic behaviors, stepping back and then entering another execution branch of the net.

ScoreSynth presents print and graphical export features, and it saves nets in PNML (Petri Net Markup Language), which is an XML-based standard interchange format used to represent PNs.

Currently, a Web-based version of *ScoreSynth* is under development at the Laboratory of Music Informatics of the University of Milan. The characteristics of the original software have been preserved, and some new features have been added (e.g., more control on the graphical layout of the net). *ScoreSynth Web Edition* does not require installation, is cross-platform and available on each device equipped with an HTML5 browser and an Internet connection. A screenshot of the interface is shown in Fig. 7.

6.2   A Block-Based Interface

The mentioned efforts go in the direction of facilitating the use of PNs and MPNs for non-expert users, but they still do not respond to the request for a user-friendly tool for musicians. In this section we will propose a browser application which aims to bridge the gap between traditional interfaces for music manipulation and MPNs, based on a block-programming paradigm. Its interface is shown in Fig. 8.

From a logical point of view, the software presents three phases: preparation of the block diagram, macro expansion, and post-processing.

The first phase focuses on the *outline of a diagram* where MOs can be placed, modified through suitable operators, and connected together as a graph. This process can be further decomposed into steps. First, MOs are loaded into the

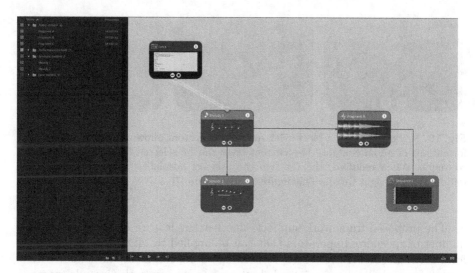

Fig. 8. The proposed interface for a block-based editor.

Fig. 9. Blocks with heterogeneous content for the proposed interface. From left to right: audio data, computer-driven performance, music notation, source code, and patch.

Object Gallery, organized by type, marked through a user-defined name (e.g., "Fragment A", "Main theme", "Chorus", etc.), and associated with a color. After the import step, MOs can be placed over the canvas by using drag-and-drop operations and connected together through cords that join outlets and inlets.

Inside the canvas, MOs are represented as rectangular blocks, identified by a name, an icon, and a conventional color that specifies the MO type. Depending on the type of content, blocks are given different graphical representations: music notation in case of symbolic content, piano roll for computer-driven performances, waveforms for audio, source code for sound and music computing system, patches for dataflow programming languages, etc. (see Fig. 9). Each rectangle embeds basic media controls to play its content; in case of non-audio blocks, an internal parser with synthesis function has to be invoked.

For each block, multiple ingoing and outgoing connections are supported. Cords may belong to two different types: a) *concurrent arcs*, represented by solid lines, meaning that all concurrent outgoing paths are traveled simultaneously, and b) *exclusive arcs*, represented by dashed lines, implying that a path excludes the others; in this case, priority is expressed through numbers over arcs, so as to obtain a sorted sequence of paths to be visited.

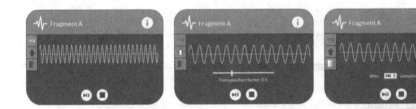

Fig. 10. Stacked tabs for a block with multiple operators, showing step-by-step transformations of audio content. The current layer can be selected in the left side of the rectangle. When required, the tab lets the user set specialized parameters (see the middle and the right tabs). This figure is taken from [7].

The proposed framework supports another key feature of MPNs, namely a number of specialized operators that can be applied to MOs in order to transform them into new MOs. Music-content operators can manipulate information concerning melodic, harmonic and rhythmic aspects; examples include transposition by a given interval, inversion, calculation of the retrograde, augmentation and diminution, etc. Audio-related content can be modified through pitch shifting, time stretching, fade-in and fade-out, filters, and other effects. In general, each kind of supported content is supposed to have an extensible set of specialized operators. Moreover, processes can be applied in a selective way (e.g., "Transpose only G-pitched eighth notes one octave below") and they can carry parameters (e.g., "Transpose all notes in the sequence by x halftones up", with $x \in \mathbb{N}$). Please note that, if no operator is invoked, the final result will be a graph of music excerpts with no modification, useful to provide a high-level description of the composition.

As shown in Sect. 4, MPN operators are typically linked to transitions: when the transition fires, the corresponding musical operator is triggered, thus modifying the MOs contained in input places and passing the transformed MOs to output places. This process, formally defined in MPN theory, is hard to understand for non-experts. For this reason, in the proposed interface also musical operators are associated with blocks, and they can be stacked one on top of the other. Blocks, carrying only music content so far, now contain tab views that allow to track step-by-step the transformations achieved by single operators. Figure 10, extracted from [7], shows a clarifying example about cascading transformations of audio content: a sine wave is first transposed one octave below (pitch shifting by a factor 0.5) and then faded out after n samples. The figure illustrates the graphical aspect of the three panels contained in the same block.

After consolidating the structure of the graph, the second phase, called *macro expansion*, can occur. The goal is to turn such a diagram into a MPN. In computer science, a macro-instruction (or simply macro) is a rule or pattern that specifies how a certain input sequence should be replaced by an output sequence according to a defined procedure. Macro expansion stands for the mapping process that instantiates a macro use into a specific sequence. Under our working hypotheses, macro expansion is easy to achieve. Each block of the original graph can be substituted by a suitable subnet. When operators have to be applied, the corresponding algorithms are implemented within transitions. Cords become arcs that join subnets together, possibly weighted by probabilistic values in order to support exclusive paths.

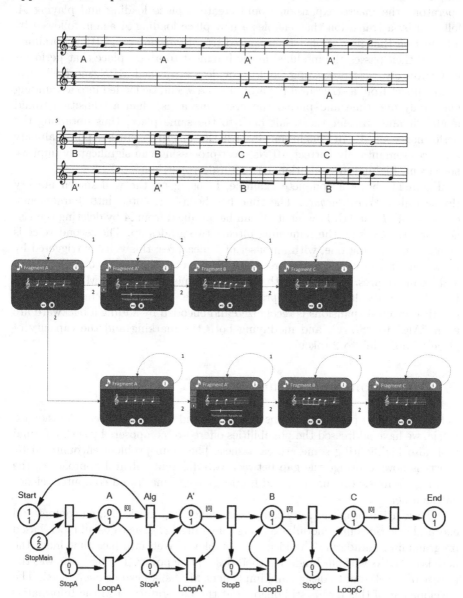

Fig. 11. Score of *Frère Jacques* (above), the corresponding graph (middle), and the underlying MPN, obtained at the end of the post-processing phase (below). This figure is taken from [7].

The third phase, called *post-processing*, works on the MPNs resulting from the previous phase and seeks for recurrent structures in order to improve their representation. For the sake of clarity, an example is called for. If in the original graph a MO called $\mathcal{A}$ is followed by $\mathcal{A}'$, obtained from $\mathcal{A}$ by applying some operators, the macro expansion would create a place loading and playing $\mathcal{A}$, followed by a transition that enables a new place loading $\mathcal{A}$ again, followed by a transition that first applies the required transformation on $\mathcal{A}$ (thus obtaining $\mathcal{A}'$) and then passes the modified music fragment to a new place that performs it. Conversely, post-processing would provide a beautified MPN, more effective and compact from a structural point of view: $\mathcal{A}$ would be loaded into a sounding place only one time and played the first time as is, than a transition would modify it and transfer the result back to the same place, thus obtaining the performance of $\mathcal{A}'$. In conclusion, even if the macro expansion phase already produces semantically correct MPNs, post-processing can significantly improve net layout, highlighting additional structural properties.

Figure 11 shows a complete example, focusing on the well-known nursery rhyme called *Frère Jacques*. The tune has been segmented into 4 fragments, called $\mathcal{A}$, $\mathcal{A}'$, $\mathcal{B}$, and $\mathcal{C}$. Fragment $\mathcal{A}'$ can be obtained from $\mathcal{A}$ by deleting the last note and transposing the remaining pitches two grades up. The second voice is identical to the first one, with an offset of 2 measures; this voice is triggered by the second instance of $\mathcal{A}$ in the first voice. Please note the use of both concurrent and exclusive arcs, the latter with a priority value. Finally, the MPN shown in Fig. 11 is the result of the post-processing phase, where the occurrence of two identical macro-expansions is recognized and encoded by adding a backward arc from "Alg" to "Start", and modifying both the marking and the capacity of place "StopMain" to 2 tokens.

7   Conclusions and Future Work

In this work, after providing details about PNs and their specialized extension for music, we have addressed the possibilities offered to composers by such a formal tool, also highlighting some critical issues. The main problem encountered by artists is how to bridge the gap between two different cultural approaches: the language of music on one side, and the language of math and computer science on the other.

The solution proposed here consists in embedding music-related content and executable actions into modular objects called blocks, so as to recall block-based programming paradigm. The idea is to employ a Web interface that hides the details of MPNs without hindering their descriptive power. The first step was the release of a web tool to design and implement MPNs, known as *ScoreSynth*. The development of this tool is still ongoing at the Laboratory of Music Informatics of the University of Milan.

ScoreSynth Web Edition is currently being tested by the students of the Bachelor's Degree in Music Informatics of the University of Milan. One of the final assignments of a lab course consists in formalizing a music piece, or a significant part of it, in terms of MPNs. This allows both to increase the corpus of available PNs and to debug the current version of the application.

Concerning future work, the goal is to implement an advanced Web editor in order to support all the features described in Sect. 6.2 and to extend managed contents to additional categories with respect to music symbols, performance information and audio data.

References

1. Assayag, G., Rueda, C., Laurson, M., Agon, C., Delerue, O.: Computer-assisted composition at IRCAM: from PatchWork to OpenMusic. Comput. Music J. **23**(3), 59–72 (1999)
2. Baggi, D., Haus, G.: IEEE 1599: music encoding and interaction. Computer **42**(3), 84–87 (2009)
3. Baggi, D.L., Haus, G.M.: Music Navigation with Symbols and Layers: Toward Content Browsing with IEEE 1599 XML Encoding. Wiley, Hoboken (2013)
4. Baldan, S., Barate, A., Ludovico, L.A.: Automatic performance of Black and White n. 2: the influence of emotions over aleatoric music. In: Proceedings of International Symposium on Computer Music Modeling and Retrieval (CMMR), pp. 437–448 (2012)
5. Baratè, A., Haus, G., Ludovico, L.A.: Music analysis and modeling through Petri nets. In: Kronland-Martinet, R., Voinier, T., Ystad, S. (eds.) CMMR 2005. LNCS, vol. 3902, pp. 201–218. Springer, Heidelberg (2006). https://doi.org/10.1007/11751069_19
6. Baratè, A., Haus, G., Ludovico, L.A.: Real-time music composition through P-timed Petri nets. In: Georgaki, A., Kouroupetroglou, G. (eds.) ICMC—SMC—2014 Proceedings, Athens 14–20 September 2014, pp. 408–415. Athens (2014)
7. Baratè, A., Haus, G., Ludovico, L.A.: Formalisms and interfaces to manipulate music information: the case of music Petri nets. In: Constantine, L., da Silva, H.P., Escalona, M.J., Helfert, M., Jimenez Ramirez, A. (eds.) Proceedings of the 2nd International Conference on Computer-Human Interaction Research and Applications (CHIRA 2018), pp. 81–90. SCITEPRESS - Science and Technology Publications, Lda (2018)
8. Baratè, A., Haus, G., Ludovico, L.A.: State of the art and perspectives in multi-layer formats for music representation. In: Proceedings of the 2019 International Workshop on Multilayer Music Representation and Processing (MMRP 2019), pp. 27–34. IEEE CPS (2019). https://doi.org/10.1109/MMRP.2019.8665381
9. Baratè, A., Haus, G., Ludovico, L.A., Mauro, D.A.: Formalizing Schoenberg's fundamentals of musical composition through Petri nets. In: Proceedings of the 15th International Sound and Music Computing Conference (SMC 2018), Limassol, Cyprus, pp. 254–258 (2018). https://doi.org/10.5281/zenodo.1422579
10. Bresson, J., Agon, C., Assayag, G.: OpenMusic: visual programming environment for music composition, analysis and research. In: Proceedings of the 19th ACM International Conference on Multimedia, pp. 743–746 (2011)
11. Brown, E.: The notation and performance of new music. Music. Q. **72**(2), 180–201 (1986)
12. Cook, P.: Principles for designing computer music controllers. In: Proceedings of the CHI 2001 Workshop on New Interfaces for Musical Expression (NIME 2001), Seattle, USA, pp. 1–6. NIME (2001)

13. David, R., Alla, H.: Petri nets for modeling of dynamic systems: a survey. Automatica **30**(2), 175–202 (1994)
14. De Matteis, A., Haus, G.: Formalization of generative structures within Stravinsky's "The Rite of Spring". J. New Music Res. **25**(1), 47–76 (1996)
15. Dingle, N.J., Knottenbelt, W.J., Suto, T.: PIPE2: a tool for the performance evaluation of generalised stochastic Petri Nets. ACM SIGMETRICS Perform. Eval. Rev. **36**(4), 34–39 (2009)
16. Frederickson, J.: Technology and music performance in the age of mechanical reproduction. Int. Rev. Aesthet. Sociol. Music **20**(2), 193–220 (1989)
17. Garcia, J., Bouche, D., Bresson, J.: Timed sequences: a framework for computer-aided composition with temporal structures. In: Third International Conference on Technologies for Music Notation and Representation (TENOR 2017), A Coruña, Spain, May 2017. https://hal.archives-ouvertes.fr/hal-01484077
18. Garcia, J., Carpentier, T., Bresson, J.: Interactive-compositional authoring of sound spatialization. J. New Music Res. **46**(1), 20 (2017). https://doi.org/10.1080/09298215.2016.1230632. https://hal.inria.fr/hal-01467080
19. Good, M.: MusicXML for notation and analysis. In: The Virtual Score: Representation, Retrieval, Restoration, vol. 12, pp. 113–124 (2001)
20. Gould, E.: Behind Bars: The Definitive Guide to Music Notation. Faber Music Ltd., London (2016)
21. Haus, G., Rodriguez, A.: Formal music representation; a case study: the model of Ravel's Bolero by Petri nets. In: Music Processing. Computer Music and Digital Audio Series, pp. 165–232 (1993)
22. Haus, G., Sametti, A.: Scoresynth: a system for the synthesis of music scores based on Petri nets and a music algebra. Computer **24**(7), 56–60 (1991)
23. Hedges, S.A.: Dice music in the eighteenth century. Music Lett. **59**(2), 180–187 (1978)
24. Jensen, K., Rozenberg, G.: High-Level Petri Nets: Theory and Application. Springer, Heidelberg (2012)
25. Jones, S.: Music that moves: popular music, distribution and network technologies. Cult. Stud. **16**(2), 213–232 (2002)
26. Kudlek, M.: Probability in Petri nets. Fundamenta Informaticae **67**(1–3), 121–130 (2005)
27. Lee, K.H., Favrel, J.: Hierarchical reduction method for analysis and decomposition of Petri nets. IEEE Trans. Syst. Man. Cybern. **SMC–15**(2), 272–280 (1985)
28. Lerdahl, F., Jackendoff, R.: An overview of hierarchical structure in music. Music Percept. **1**(2), 229–252 (1983)
29. Lerdahl, F., Jackendoff, R.S.: A Generative Theory of Tonal Music. MIT Press, Cambridge (1985)
30. Lin, C., Marinescu, D.C.: Stochastic high-level Petri nets and applications. In: Jensen, K., Rozenberg, G. (eds.) High-level Petri Nets, pp. 459–469. Springer, Heidelberg (1988). https://doi.org/10.1007/978-3-642-84524-6_16
31. Miranda, E.R., Kirby, S., Todd, P.: On computational models of the evolution of music: from the origins of musical taste to the emergence of grammars. Contemp. Music Rev. **22**(3), 91–111 (2003)
32. Molloy, M.K.: Discrete time stochastic Petri nets. IEEE Trans. Software Eng. **SE–11**(4), 417–423 (1985)
33. Paradiso, J.A., O'Modhrain, S.: Current trends in electronic music interfaces. J. New Music Res. **32**(4), 345–349 (2003)
34. Pennycook, B.W.: Computer-music interfaces: a survey. ACM Comput. Surv. (CSUR) **17**(2), 267–289 (1985)

35. Peterson, J.L.: Petri nets. ACM Comput. Surv. (CSUR) **9**(3), 223–252 (1977)
36. Petri, C.A.: Introduction to general net theory. In: Brauer, W. (ed.) Net Theory and Applications. LNCS, vol. 84, pp. 1–19. Springer, Heidelberg (1980). https://doi.org/10.1007/3-540-10001-6_21
37. Pritchett, J.: The Music of John Cage, vol. 5. Cambridge University Press, Cambridge (1996)
38. Puckette, M., et al.: Pure Data: another integrated computer music environment. In: Proceedings of the Second Intercollege Computer Music Concerts, pp. 37–41 (1996)
39. Ramchandani, C.: Analysis of asynchronous concurrent systems by timed Petri nets. Ph.D. thesis, Massachusetts Institute of Technology (1973)
40. Roland, P.: The music encoding initiative (MEI). In: Proceedings of the First International Conference on Musical Applications Using XML, vol. 1060, pp. 55–59. IEEE (2002)
41. Sachs, C.: The History of Musical Instruments. Courier Corporation, North Chelmsford (2012)
42. Schoenberg, A.: Models for Beginners in Composition. G. Schinner, Inc., New York (1942)
43. Schoenberg, A., Stein, L., Strang, G.: Fundamentals of Musical Composition. Faber & Faber, London (1967)
44. Serafin, S., Erkut, C., Kojs, J., Nilsson, N.C., Nordahl, R.: Virtual reality musical instruments: state of the art, design principles, and future directions. Comput. Music J. **40**(3), 22–40 (2016)
45. Talbot, P., Agon, C., Esling, P.: Interactive computer-aided composition with constraints. In: 43rd International Computer Music Conference (ICMC 2017), Shanghai, China, October 2017. https://hal.archives-ouvertes.fr/hal-01577898
46. Vinjar, A., Bresson, J.: OM-AI: a toolkit to support AI-based computer-assisted composition workflows in OpenMusic. In: 16th Sound and Music Computing conference (SMC 2019), Málaga, Spain (2019). https://hal.archives-ouvertes.fr/hal-02126847
47. Wang, J.: Timed Petri Nets: Theory and Application, vol. 9. Springer, Boston (2012). https://doi.org/10.1007/978-1-4615-5537-7
48. Zicarelli, D.D.: An extensible real-time signal processing environment for Max. In: Proceedings of the International Computer Music Conference, vol. 98, pp. 463–466 (1992)
49. Zuberek, W.M.: Timed Petri nets definitions, properties, and applications. Microelectron. Reliab. **31**(4), 627–644 (1991)

Through the Looking Glass: Designing Agents for MAS Based Shape-Shifting Technology Using the STEAM Approach

Helen Hasenfuss$^{(\boxtimes)}$ (iD)

Abbeyfeale, Co., Limerick, Ireland
helenh2009@gmail.com

Abstract. The aim of this paper is to explore the development of shape shifting technology through the development of the Dod. The Dod is an agent design which was developed as part of a PhD study completed in 2018. It represents an attempt to close the gap between the copious research on agent behavior and communication and the sparse development of a physical design (i.e. a body) that will eventually contain the agent's behavior mechanism. This exploration will cover how the Dod's development (multifunction/purpose), strongly guided by the STEAM (Science, Technology, Engineering, Arts, Mathematics) approach, is appropriate to adapting into future applications. An important result of this study is the recognition for the importance of developing multidisciplinary experts. Designing shape-shifting technology requires knowledge of many different fields and in order to create viable design blueprints, it is necessary for designers to learn to acquire, understand and apply knowledge from a diverse range of subjects.

Keywords: STEAM · Shape-shifting technology · MAS design · Agent

1 Introduction

This paper is an extension of the conference paper, Reinventing the Cube.... presented at CHIRA conference in 2019 [2]. In that paper the physical design of an agent is described: the Dod. This design is envisioned to progress the study of multiagent systems (MAS) in their use in shape-shifting technology, which is most often portrayed via many small parts operating together to create a larger entity. The individual parts are referred to as agents and are autonomous entities. They can be represented physically (organic or artificial structure) or digitally and an important quality of each agent is its ability to learn and make decisions based on its behavioural coding.

The Dod is based on the shape of a dodecahedron, with the addition of being able to extend arms from all of its 12 facets. The arms take the shape of an inverted fustrum and have 2 states: fully retracted and fully extended. The six characteristics or qualities

---

In reference to Lewis Carrol's novel whereby Alice crosses into a universe where things are not what they seem and where the unpredictable happens [1]. An apt description for the approach needed to solve problems without knowing all the facts.

© Springer Nature Switzerland AG 2021
M. J. Escalona et al. (Eds.): CHIRA 2018/CHIRA 2019, CCIS 1351, pp. 80–101, 2021.
https://doi.org/10.1007/978-3-030-67108-2_5

that emerged through the research, that had a direct impact on the physical design of the Dod, are as follows:

- A semi-spherical shape with an irregular, cratered surface.
- Non-hierarchical chain of command: autonomy to function as individuals
- The ability to morph: surface topology and fundamental form
- One material make-up and scalability – structural affordances and inherent material qualities
- Bi-directionality – the ability to assemble and dis-assembly
- Behavioural simplicity

The development of the Dod reflects an important consideration that was part of the original research question: instead of creating another fully functioning prototype that could only exist in a lab environment [3–7], it was important to consider a diverse range of applications both in the present and future. The Dod design, as well as the process used to achieve it, incorporate the possibility of accommodating future shifts in technological developments (e.g. biological 3D printing, electrospinning). The aim was to generate a viable blueprint for an agent design that is applicable in the present and future. This paper will delve further into elements of the design process used to develop the Dod. These elements provide a roadmap for the scope of Design as a multidisciplinary subject but also demonstrate the possibility to develop designers as multidisciplinary experts.

Section two will present a brief summary of related work to contextualise the research in the field of Tangible Interfaces and establish the premise on which the discussion in this paper is based.

The STEAM method or approach used to facilitate the Dod's development, will be presented in greater detail in section three. Even though it can be argued that there is inherent creativity in the STEM disciplines, primarily through the inclusion of mathematics, the quality and nature of creativity relies on the diverse forms of its expression. Creativity represents a persons physical output or contribution but also the emotional component involved in its application.

Examples of the original study will be used to demonstrate how the STEAM approach was beneficial and can help to develop the multidisciplinary skills that are essential to help create designs with unknown variables. These examples will be illustrated in section four.

Section five will elaborate further on how specific theoretical guidelines emerged through the STEAM approach and the difference they made to the resulting design of the Dod. Specific reference to the philosophy of multidisciplinary design will be addressed. A challenge of design research is to evenly balance the resulting output with the philosophy. In the case of the Dod, because some variables in the design process were unknown it was important to draw knowledge from a subject that can handle unexpected outcomes and random occurrences: aesthetics.

2   Related Work

The Dod was developed within the parameters of the Tangible Interface (TI) classification scheme as defined by Ishii and Ulmer [8], specifically the category of constructed assemblies and continuous plastic TUIs. The Dod is designed so that it is not only the individual agent topology that can change shape but that of the whole interface once many of these agents work together. This behaviour creates a sub category to continuous plastic TUIs, whereby users can interact with a malleable and adaptable building material with which to manipulate digital information. The agent's morphing abilities facilitate the generation of micro structures which are central to the overall assembly process. These micro structures include a line, curve, or cluster. Whilst serving a functional purpose on the micro level (i.e. building structures and aiding agent self-assembly), these structures serve a practical purpose on the macro level, in that it utilises the full potential of the haptic modality, creating varied surface textures. The morphing of individual agents can be used to explore the textural scope of a shape-shifting interface, e.g. the overall interface need not change however the surface texture can be reactive to a variety of elements such as sound, temp, users galvanic skin response, etc. Similar behaviours are evident in SMA or push-pin based interfaces [5, 9, 10]. These types of interfaces combine programmable matter concepts with ambient computing, generating interfaces that are more reactive to the individual user or their environment. This reactiveness is a key component that emulates the unique haptic characteristic of bi-directionality. This quality makes it possible to react to and also act on sensory information [11–14].

2.1 Key Qualities of Haptics

Whilst computer interfaces have explored and integrated the visual and aural senses with a variety of different products, the Dod study falls into the category of haptic interfaces. The tactile sense grounds a person in reality and assists in creating a 3D holistic impression of the world [13]. This quality of grounding can be combined with other senses to facilitate the practical and emotional aspects of interaction [15, 16]. For example, a rough, spiked surface may indicate that an error has occurred or fast pulsating vibration may indicate an alarm and similarly a slow, fluid transition between interfaces can calmly guide a user through a sequence of steps. A key difference in the design of future haptic interfaces is the concept of dynamic design, that the original design is no longer static, like a mouse or keyboard. Instead, more ownership is handed to the user with respect to creating malleable tangible user interfaces (TUIs). Similar to hearing, it is not possible to stop feeling however it is possible to temporarily stop receiving information, in some instances, by inertness. For example, to feel texture, vibration, or force, etc. requires the user to move over a surface, or to push or pull the object. If a user touches an object but does not move or exert a force then there is no new information being transmitted. This concept is being explored and also translated into different fields, e.g. energy efficiency. Tactus technology create overlay screens, which enable buttons to rise out of the surface once a keyboard or buttons are detected on the flat screen below. This is based on the technology of microfluidics and can be adapted for different screen setups and styles [17]. BlueMotion™ technology in cars demonstrates how energy is not used until it is required [18, 19]. Many haptic interactive interfaces are still at a prototyping stage, are cumbersome and lab based due to the expertise and equipment required to keep them operational. The concept and appeal of the MAS is that it can be self-contained and that the agents are autonomous not only in their behavioural ability but also in their sustainability. An appeal in haptic interfaces is the multimodal sensing quality that is inherent in these interfaces. Haptic sensing rarely occurs in isolation, i.e. it is an intrinsic part of a multi-modal sensory system of perception [3, 20, 21]. If two or more senses are working simultaneously at interpreting the same situation there is more information on which to base a decision [22–24]. As some senses have a higher weighted priority than others, which can often lead to false perceptions or a masking of the other senses [11, 14, 22, 25], the combination of vision and haptics is advantageous.

2.2 Design Roadmap

With respect to designing haptic interfaces, the roadmap to Multimedia Haptics described by Saddik is informative [14]. It describes the interdependence of each component and how the development of one area depends on the knowledge and understanding of other components linked to it. Figure 1, illustrates an adapted version of the multimedia roadmap with the addition of specific elements that emerged through the early stages of prototyping agent designs in the original study of the Dod [26]. These elements include a) power supplies to the domain of Machine Haptics, b) latency to the domain of computer haptics and c) the branch of extraneous factors. Considering how energy is input and manipulated in a shape-shifting system is a critical consideration with respect to the agent's physical design. The original conference paper illustrates several considerations of energy supplies ranging from chemical or biological processes to symbiotic relationships [2]. A discrepancy between action and reaction (latency) interferes with a user's connection and perception between interface and task. A good analogy is Mark Weiser's description of an invisible tool. The tool itself should be intuitive and easy to learn and so natural to use that the focus and attention of the user is directed towards the task itself rather than be distracted by the implement used to carry out the task [27]. The complete branch of extraneous factors- illustrates elements that have varied priority weights throughout an interface design process, however should be considered and included on an ongoing basis as they impact on the design.

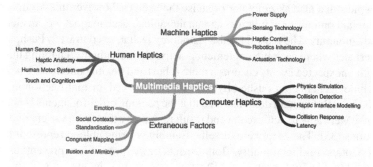

Fig. 1. Multimedia Haptics - Elements and considerations that influence multimedia design.

2.3 Systems

Considering the elements described in the multimedia haptic roadmap provides a good starting point for developing haptic interfaces. Several styles of interface addressing these issues were explored and detailed in the original paper (1). These include pushpin computing and smart/Non-Newtonian fluid-based interfaces. The Dod is based on the 3rd type of shape-shifting technique: MAS. A MAS is a freestanding system, which are pervasive through nearly all levels of existence, e.g. individual cells working together, a flock of birds, the stock market, solar system, etc. With respect to artificial MAS, these interfaces consist of modular agents, i.e. they are structurally identical to each other. Thereby the haptic component is inherent in their makeup in either of two ways: A) in the physical handling of each individual component (e.g. a tile) [28, 29] or B) in the physical handling of the overall system created by many small parts. A unique quality of modular interfaces is the ability to add and subtract agents [15, 28]. This presents a unique challenge with respect to communication between each component. Distributed sensor networks [30–32] or self–organisation models are applied to create an adaptable and flexible system. From a haptic perspective, these systems have a greater emphasis on kinaesthetic since the interfaces are completely 3D [29, 33]. The peripheral technology, that is necessary for pushpin and smart fluid interfaces, is primarily intrinsic to each agent. The emphasis of a MAS is on agent autonomy, which means a large portion of academic research has been invested into developing the process of self-assembly itself and that of agent-to-agent communication.

Self-assembly, more so than self-organisation, is an essential ability for a MAS that is envisioned to create 3D TUIs. It includes the aspects of agent packing and orientation, that is inherent in the latter term [34, 35], however it also includes the process of agents being able to connect to each other in order to form macro structures. For a shape-shifting, autonomous MAS dynamic self-assembly is required [36]. Dynamic self-assembly is often evident in biological systems. It indicates a cooperation and communication between agents to achieve a specific goal. For example, the manner in which ants can assemble to create structures such as bridges or rafts, etc. [37]. Compared to a set of ball magnets that also assemble or organise themselves, however this occurs according to the polar configuration inherent and unalterable to each magnet, i.e. an element of choice and autonomy. The reason for this autonomy is that, in contrast to Pushpin Computing interfaces where each pin or element is activated individually, enabling the agents to cope with unexpected events ensures a more robust and flexible interface. Unexpected events include agents being pushed by each other, removed, or malfunctioning. In the project *Kilobots*, Rubenstein demonstrated that the packing order for agents is not necessary, i.e. they were able to achieve the end result repeatedly through a variety of different configurations [35]. The advantage of self-assembly is being able to represent the core quality of haptics: bi-directionality. Both aspects of the process are present: assembly and disassembly. Ideally for tangible MAS this process must happen in real-time. Similar to many areas of research, the source of the initial inspiration for how this type of shape-shifting, haptic interface was found in the biological domain: ant, bee and termite hives. Because of this, biomimetics had a strong influence in the research for developing the Dod and continued to be regular reference point as the design requirements for the Dod developed. Each of these complex colonies can have an excess of several thousand living beings, however each individual has its own task and is appropriately equipped to carry out this task [38, 39]. The manner in which these insects communicate and interact and the scale at which they exist provided valuable design insights. Projects such as Bergbreiter's mini jumping robots [40] and *microTug* [41] represent progress with respect to scaling mechanical system. However, wear, stress and strain still limit the lifespan of inorganic systems. The primary biological source of inspiration for the Dod agent, was the *Solenopsis Invicta* (fire ants). Due to their natural habitat being prone to flooding, these ants have adapted by being able to build temporary rafts until they find a new area of land. The raft consists entirely of ants, which demonstrates that they can maintain structural cohesion, buoyancy and can survive temporary submergence in water. They also demonstrate behaviour similar to Non-Newtonian fluids: when agitated, e.g. swirled in a beaker, they maintain a semi-spherical shape and when left alone begin to disperse again over time, etc.) [42].

Whilst biological systems provide an abundance of information regarding agent-to-agent interaction, focus on the agent's physical body has been neglected. A problem in designing the body of the agent lies in the unknown end application of shape-shifting technology:

- Defining how this type of interface should be used?
- In which environment it will be?
- How humans will actually interact with it?
- What it should look, feel, or sound like?
- How intelligent it needs to be?

This paper aims to demonstrate how using the STEAM approach can aid the process of design when dealing with unknown variable. In doing so the need for designers to be adept in the skill of applying an active dialogue between inductive and deductive reasoning is illustrated. Whilst the interplay between scientific and artistic methodologies may occur, it is often not actively documented. For example, to develop a haptic interface, haptic exploration of textures, shape, size, form, temperature, etc. is as integral to help develop the functionality of the interface.

3 Methodology

The STEAM method or approach applied in the development of the Dod is an amalgamation of scientific procedures and art-based design methods. A single STEAM method cannot be clearly delineated, only so far as that STEM methodologies can be used to test hypothesis and that Art methodologies can be used to generate these hypotheses. This section will elaborate how the STEAM approach was used to assist in the design process of the Dod.

Since specific or unique applications for shape-shifting technologies do not yet exist (i.e. the suggested applications are primarily augmentations or replacements of existing interfaces), it is necessary to design in order to accommodate for unknown applications. The general design brief for shape-shifting interfaces that has emerged through art and academic research are as follows:

- It can change shape according to the user's requirements
- Shape changes should occur in real-time
- It should react to the user
- It should provide a variety of textural and haptic responses, possibly even become personalized to each individual user.

Potential applications of this type of technology have most successfully been explore in a creative and intangible: through film [43–47]. The general MAS concept was also reflected in these environments. Processing and exploring this technology through film provides valuable insight into how such new and unique technology can theoretically function or the ideal application. These suggestions address aspects of creativity, ingenuity, uniqueness and aesthetics. They are less insightful regarding the practical aspects such as cohesion, communication, physical construction, energy manipulation, constructive self-assembly, production, etc. The design challenge in the research of this technology combining these two separate interpretations. In academia, the STEAM approach can be applied to foster the skills to research and design within the gap between creativity and logic. Similar to the need for professionals that have a singular expertise in a particular field, it is necessary to train professionals that have an expertise in intelligently encompassing a variety of fields: a multidisciplinary professional.

STEAM is the incorporation of Arts into the STEM disciplines. Similar to Science in that the term itself describes many sub categories in this discipline (e.g. physics, biology, microfluidics, quantum theory, etc.), Art also covers a variety of categories other than drawing, sculpting, poetry, dancing, music, etc.). It covers subjects such as philosophy, and phenomenology- many of which attempt to deal with aspect of humanity that are still intangible and to a degree undefined. For example, through psychology it is possible to determine where creativity occurs in the human brain and to test whether it exists in other animals. However, the essence of how creativity is interpreted and why it is done so in that particular way can be analyzed in phenomenology. Perception is unique to each individual and whilst this quality does not have a high priority in the STEM methodologies, it is necessary in the domain of design. The addition of artistic methodologies in the design process of the Dod created space for a shift in research focus to occur, allowing for aesthetics, imagination, improvisation and creativity to take higher priority and thereby increasing the scope of the design. Intuition plays a stronger, more present role in the art domain because this domain facilitates the experiential and creative aspect of a person. Even though intuition is also present in the science domains it is not usually applied as a means of proof, but more so a means of providing an initial starting point of research or investigation. Experiments and specific procedures exist as part of the scientific methodology in order to provide rigorous and repeatable results. Art is intrinsically a subjective and practical domain, therefore the majority of research from this area is presented in one of three ways, A) an artwork, B) the process itself is the artwork, or C) the work is a purely philosophical, written expression [48]. There are not many clearly defined frameworks for presenting the artists' research process therefore defining the artistic methodology is at times problematic. In its nature, Art allows individuals to question and push the boundaries of established procedures and institutions. For example, Paul Feyerabend believed that the unvarying, objective approach present in scientific methodologies had become restrictive and unyielding. He suggested a subjective, more intuitive approach to articulating research findings [48]. This approach essentially enables the researchers to personalize the method by which he/she has attained the end results and emphasizes that it is a reflection on the process itself not the outcome that constitutes the significant research.

Methodological diversity and flexibility are encouraged within the creative disciplines [49] as maintaining unstructured methodology is a contribution of artistic research in itself. As an example, consider the initial struggle of the psychology discipline to be taken seriously in the academic community. Researchers in psychology began to employ and adapt scientific methodologies in order to gain acceptance and recognition. Whilst it can be argued that it has achieved part of this goal, the question that arises is, whether the discipline has maintained its inherent integrity? In the attempt of researchers to conform to methodologies of other established disciplines, that are contrary to their own, the risk of losing the integral meaning and concept of the discipline in question exists. Attempting to clearly define and organize an artistic method comes from a scientific or logical perspective or orientation, i.e. the desire to structure and order knowledge. However similar to the concept embodied by the 1916 Dadaism movement, sometimes it may be necessary to accept that certain research methods have to maintain a peripheral or intangible status as opposed to an acutely focused one. In relation to Dadaism, as people (academics, critics, artists, etc.) attempted to clearly define and describe what Dadaism actually represented and meant, the more elusive and dissipated the movement's meaning became. While the scientific disciplines remain relatively constant because of their derivations from objectivity and logic, the arts and humanities reflect the Zeitgeist of the period, the artists phenomenology and the versatility to adapt to creativity. The openness and less stringent boundary conditions of the arts ensures a space for creative exploration and engagement.

A STEAM method is usually individually crafted for specific design projects because it not only accommodates a testing procedure, which is still necessary and usually scientific based, but it also integrates the researcher as a person, their strengths, skills and interpretations. The Dod reflects aspects of biomimicry, aesthetics, physical affordances, potential to evolve, geometry, physics, and origami. The need for design researchers to exercise skills in diversifying becomes apparent.

The design of the Dod used the principles of User Centered Design (UCD) except that the user is replaced by a dialogue of inductive (e.g. creativity) and deductive (e.g. logic) reasoning. The terms top-down and bottom-up, although used in a variety of disciplines, can be used as analogies to represent the complex processing or reasoning concepts that are inherent in inductive and deductive reasoning. For example, inductive reasoning can be described using the bottom-up analogy. Bottom-up encompasses working from existing knowledge and building upon this base to accomplish a specific goal or understanding. It is a process whereby the small parts sum together to make the complete whole. In inductive reasoning, the premises that define the argument are specific and enable the process of making observations and pattern-finding until it is eventually possible to formulate hypotheses which in term inform a generalized theory. The conclusions drawn from inductive reasoning are based on the evidence of the premises more so that the actual premise itself. It means that these conclusions promote a probability as opposed to a clear certainty and that even if all the premises are correct, it is still possible for the conclusions to be false. The more data that is available in the construction of the premises ensures a greater probability that the conclusions will be true. In contrast, the top-down approach is similar to reverse engineering. The technique is based upon knowing or understanding the overall system and de-constructing it in order to gain insight to specific functions or mechanisms. Deductive reasoning has formed a standard basis for the scientific methodology and is analogous to the top-down concept. In this style of reasoning the premises are known to be true and therefore the conclusion follows logically and is also considered to be true. Unlike the conclusion reached via inductive inference, deductive conclusions are formed as a logical progressions or experiments from the original premises. This means that even if the premises are incorrect the conclusion would still be logical.

The advantage of a STEAM method in the situation of designing a product with unknown variables is that the creative subjects usually have a better capacity to deal with the unknown or improvisation. Whilst it is not possible to design for all eventualities, there is a greater possibility of designing such that certain elements have sub functions or affordances that become relevant at a later stage. The focus of design is not solely on the known design parameters. For example, the shape and construction of the individual Dod allows it to be useful with the system, even if it would potentially suffer complete malfunction. This affordance can be used to counteract the current 'throw-away' attitude to technology, e.g. if specific components of a laptop are broken beyond repair, the entire laptop is usually scrapped by the average user as repairs are often too expensive. This approach is wasteful and detrimental to the environment, something society can no longer afford. Designing technology that can be reusable, even if several components or mechanisms fail, aims to help change the attitude to technology whilst simultaneously creating a more robust and efficient system. Considering issues such as the longevity of technology, the ability of systems to self-repair efficiently or the connection between technology and user are important design considerations even though they may seem at this point to be secondary issues from the core design process.

The following section will illustrate how a focus on aesthetics influenced the design of the Dod. Four experimental artworks were created as part of the original study. Two of these works were made as part of independent exhibitions whilst the latter two were exploring specific behaviors of the shape and movable elements used to define the Dod. These artworks can also be compared to prototypes, however the main difference being that rather than progressing a design to reach a high-fidelity stage, they provided inspirations and basic proof-of-concepts which was sufficient to continue postulating further design elements.

4 Delving into STEAM

The first part of this section will be building upon the brief introductory description of the Dod, to provide context of how this agent design is envisioned to function. The Dod is designed to accommodate the extension of 12 arms that are attached to an inner core dodecahedron. Each arm/spring is potentially encased by a membrane, see Figure X. This membrane can be semi-permeable, dense, elastic, rigid, etc. depending requirement and application. Its function was explored in relation to energy generation through triboelectricity or through the generation of chemical gradients in the original conference paper [2]. The arm mechanism is based on a pentagonal origami spring and suitably conveys the rotational extension behavior of the arm. Origami is a relevant technique that is gaining a growing research interest with respect to its ability to change shape, structure and strength [50–54]. There are several characteristics that make this art form very appealing in the robotic and interface domain:

- Changeable surface topology,
- Ability to morph shape & form,
- Auxetic quality,
- Strength transformation through structural rearrangement.
- Vast range of suitable construction materials
- Maintains qualities through scaling
- Scalable (Macro to micro structures)

The ability to extend and retract the arms is to create the topographical changes on the agent itself. Through different configurations of the arms a straight line (e.g. in a retracted state when two opposite arms are extended a straight-line structure is generated), curve and cluster can also be formed. In previous studies and prototypes of MAS based interfaces, the cube was sufficient in creating lines and clusters however due to the nature of its shape curves are not as easily constructed.

The Dod artworks are a form of abstract prototyping that has been invaluable as a means of continuously adding creative approaches and perspectives to the Dod's design. The experimentation with materials and direct form-manipulation, through the practical process of building the artworks, involves applied lateral thinking, spatial exploration and haptic contextualization. Expanding the materials and themes under which the Dod can be interpreted, not only provides interesting insights but also works towards maintaining an accessible link between research and the public through art [55]. Newly emerging professions such as *Science Communicator* highlight the importance of bringing highly abstracted concepts to accessible levels. This process stimulates discussion, thought and further ideas emanating from outside a research lab environment. It also crucially contributes to widening the perspective through which research such as this study is viewed [56].

Four different artworks exploring the Dod were constructed, reflecting the different stages of research and progress of the Dod design as a viable alternative to the cube, to be used in MAS based interfaces.

4.1 Steampunk Dod

The first Dod made in the series of Dod artworks is a Steampunk interpretation. Steampunk is a style that uses technology from the Victorian era and juxtaposes it alongside modern applications and materials. It appropriates materials for purposes that it was not initially designed or planned for. The main materials used are copper and Perspex. There are three layers of dodecahedra of increasing size, suspended within each other. The first layer consists of turned copper wire into pentagonal spirals, the second layer is of pentagons made of crocheted copper wire, and the outer layers is made from pentagons cut from perspex and embossed copper plates, see Fig. 2. Each layer is sewn together with copper wire. The work is fractal in nature and was created at the early stages of research and reflects the close imitation of the basic dodecahedron shape.

Fig. 2. Steampunk Dod - Finished artwork.

4.2 Origami Dod

The origami Dod explored the material of paper in its ability to change size, shape and strength depending on the form it is in. This is the basis of origami and like the copper wire in the previous project, taking these materials beyond their original designed function can lead to new applications but also reinventions of the material itself. The artwork plays again on the concept of a core dodecahedron being suspended in the middle of a larger dodecahedron. The outer layer consists of stenciling and iris folding whilst the inner layer consists of transparent foil, see Fig. 3c. The foil is manipulated such that it holds together without an additional substance (e.g. glue of tape). Its construction echoes certain qualities of tensegrity structures regarding a finely tuned balance between tension and form, see Fig. 3d.

(a)   **(b)**   **(c)**   **(d)**

Fig. 3. (a) and (b) Finished artwork from an external & internal perspective (c) iris folding (d) inner suspended perspex Dod.

4.3 String Dod

This Dod reflects the latest prototype with extending arms and the origami spring. The aim of this work is to A) demonstrate the functioning extending and retracting arms and B) illustrate that it is possible to have an outer 'skin' surrounding the spring without significant interference to the inner spring, as well as neighboring arm space. Since the arms are never completely retracted (due to the larger outer plates) a hollow space is created between the outer plates and the inner structure whereby the potential exists to use denser possibly bulkier materials for the skin. There is sufficient space to accommodate the excess material when in a retracted state. This 'skin', may be useful in furthering the development of the Dod's design in relation to the arm structure. It may act as a boundary between the inner arm structure and the external environment, e.g. a semi-permeable membrane.

There is an inner core in this artwork that is 3D printed in white PLA to which a pentagonal, origami spring can be attached and it can be sewn around to attach to the outer facet. A flat circular magnet is located in the center of each plate so that when the viewer holds a magnet over this plate it will extend the arm, Fig. 4. 31a. Reversing the polarity of the magnet will cause the arm to retract.

(a)   **(b)**   **(c)**   **(d)**

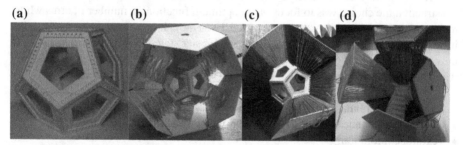

Fig. 4. (a) Inner PLA core (b) and (c) internal structure without & with 'skin' membrane (d) Final String Dod.

4.4 Latch Dod

A factor that became apparent in the study of previous agent body designs is that researchers chose a familiar shape: the cube. In an attempt to consider the value of a familiarity of form through social permeation, this Dod was created from the perspective of game or toy design. It reflects the adaptability of the design, with the potential for a diverse range of present and future applications. The artwork aims to illustrate a possible type of user behavior envisioned for a Dod used in a game capacity: to press a facet of the Dod and that it extends smoothly, see Fig. 5c. An origami pattern for a pentagonal frustum spring made it possible to maintain the concept of facet and arm rotation whilst a latch spring was located inside the origami spring itself, see Fig. 5a- b.

The observations attained from these artworks assisted in the developing a more wholistic concept of how the Dod can function as an agent in shapeshifting technology.

(a)   **(b)**   **(c)**

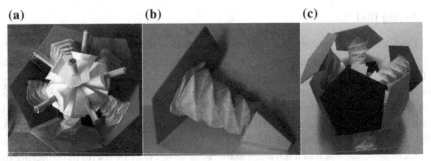

Fig. 5. (a) Spring latches contained in the inner core (b) single core-arm construction (c) Final Latch Dod.

For example, an initial consideration was to have all twelve arms movable and able to extend and retract, in order to have the maximum number of configurations possible. However, it emerged that it may not be necessary or practical to have a maximum number of configurations. The String Dod experienced a lack of structural cohesion with twelve moveable arms, therefore seven were sewn together. Perhaps in an environment with less gravity it may be possible to have twelve arms moving, however, in the current construction the choice was to focus on an optimum functioning number of arms whilst maintaining enough stability to exist unaided. Even though seven arms were made static, it was still possible to create a line, curve and cluster state through the arms that were movable. The concept of allowing the inner core of the Dod to be able to shift slightly would assist in creating a weighted behaviour, favouring specific configurations.

- Strength in combination (crocheting, layering)
- Cohesion in connection and structure (tensegrity structures)
- Textural exploration
- Moveable core to facilitate specific configurations (weighted dice)
- Arm membrane.
- Variable environment (gravity, density, temp)

Thinking and exploring the Dod in this capacity is an expression of the STEAM approach, in particular highlighting the multidisciplinary rather than interdisciplinary nature of the design process. The next section will discuss the philosophical application of the STEAM approach to the Dod's development and will end by tying each component that illustrates how the design process of the Dod is in itself an accumulation of many smaller parts to create the larger whole.

5   Discussion

It could be argued that STEAM is a more natural state of research and exploration [57] and that STEM emerged in an attempt to define and clarify a structure to handling and interpreting data. Aside from creativity and phenomenology, another important element that has a low priority in the STEM disciplines is belief. In STEM, the original intuition, belief or question of the researcher or scientist may provide the basis or reason for research but it will be rare to see a result in science, based a person's belief. Experiments will be completed in an attempt to make a belief tangible. Whilst this method is valid and necessary, it is also important to acknowledge that the strength of a person's belief can be as strong as the truest fact. Belief is often valid enough reason for many people to behave, perceive or even act in a certain manner. It is fundamental to each person and in conjunction with the filter through which they chose to carry out their research, helps create the diverse and wholesome knowledge currently in existence. All the subjects, humans chose to affiliate with or develop an expertise in, provide a unique perspective. Being able to shift perspective, and explore a problem from different subjects is an essential skill in becoming a multidisciplinary designer. Working in the gap generated by specializations within each individual subject, not only means learning about that subject but being able to understand enough in order to apply the knowledge appropriately. Whilst the physical agent design was based on a shift to aesthetics, the following texts were pivotal in defining the philosophy of the Dod's development.

Consider the concept in quantum physics that the polarization of a specific particle is determined through observation. Imagine how this is applicable to genius and insanity. Is it possible that they occupy the same space and time and that depending on the outcome of an idea or experiment, will be regarded as a success or failure?

"*What I cannot create, I do not understand*" – Richard Feynman [58]. The reverse is also applicable – a concept that is not understood cannot be adapted, shaped or reused to suit other purposes. In developing the Dod, a clear distinction is made between replication & emulation. Even though the difference between these two concepts is subtle, it is sufficient to propagate throughout a system and substantially alter the final outcome.

When an element, system or process is inspected through an acute focus, it is possible to change how it is perceived. Hofstadter illustrates this process in his use of micro-domains. The intense focus enables the researcher to gain access to alternative perspectives which in turn help to understand how each system variable functions:

"*less impressive than real world domains, the fact that they are explicitly idealised worlds allows the issues under study to be thrown into clear relief – something that generally speaking is not possible in a full-scale real-world problem.*"- [59].

What these three influential ideas have in common, among other elements, is *perspective*. It is also the reason why they are visually represented in this manner. Even though the medium of writing is sequential and linear, the process of research is generally non-linear. Different strands of research usually run in parallel or can occur in disjointed bursts. The manner in which *perspective* is approached and applied can yield insights that are as valuable as those achieved through purely scientific experimentation. *Perspective* is inherent in every piece of research but inevitably it occasionally becomes obscured. An example that demonstrates the impact of *perspective*, is Buckminster Fuller's presentation of the Dymaxion Map. It was the first map of its kind to represent the world's landmasses with greater accuracy. Due to its unique geometric division, it is possible to rearrange individual sections to present different emphasis. For example, when Fuller was requested to demonstrate the Dymaxion map to state officials, e.g. British government, he presented it in such a way that the country of origin, of the state officials, was placed in the center. In demonstrating the map to Australian officials,

Australia was placed in the center of the map and the rest of the world was arranged around it accordingly, Fig. 6 [60].

Fig. 6. Dymaxion Map - (top) land configuration (bottom) ocean configuration.

The ability to change *perspective* is powerful because it is capable of influencing thoughts and decisions, even on a subconscious level. The difficulty with *perspective* is that it is built upon a person's past experiences, knowledge and thoughts which means that no two perspectives are identical. Multi-perspectives are an inherent quality of the STEAM approach because moving between a variety of different disciplines means adapting to the unique methodology and approach of each discipline, e.g. mathematics, 3D modelling, biology, art, etc. Being able to interrupt and reassemble these inherent *perspectives*, via the techniques of microdomains or altering boundary conditions, creates the possibility of seeing alternative elements in information that may initially be overlooked. An example of this approach is commonly used in mathematics, physics, fluid- and aero-dynamics, among other subjects, whereby an *ideal condition set* is defined [61]. It represents a controllable situation and one, to which other scenarios can be compared to. It aids in the understanding of all the possible variables that can potentially affect the system and enables researchers to model the system. It is important to note that at this point, the modelled system usually cannot exist in reality. For example, the exploration of a water droplet is first modelled in the absence of variables such as gravity, friction, orientation, interaction and other forces. Boundary conditions are modelled accordingly to a weightless and contactless environment – it is the 'perfect' state or the ideal state in which the system or object can be modelled. It is not influenced by external factors that could impact on its internal structures and it is possible to decipher the fundamental variables required for existence in this particular state. Once this *ideal condition set* is established, it is then possible to begin altering variables to model the system, as it exists in reality. In a computer simulation of a particle system, physics (such as gravity, friction, viscosity, density, etc.) can be added independently to varying degrees of accuracy via [digital] physics libraries, e.g. Havok or Box2D. Whilst it is important to consider that these libraries are approximations of physical forces, i.e. models of models, their usefulness lies in being able to explore proof-of-concepts, in a research setting. Adding peripheral or independent variables to a system's fundamental variables and adjusting them, until the results replicate a variety of outcomes seen in the natural world. This enables researchers to understand their effect and relationship to the fundamental variables. It can enable researchers to clarify that even if variables correlate to each other, that it does not necessarily mean that one is the cause of the other.

The *ideal condition set* concept is integral to the development of the Dod agent because it creates the scope for the agent to be designed out of context. The interesting aspect of this process is that since the final agent design emerged from a primarily aesthetic approach and did not previously exist (i.e. it is a new and unique design), the *ideal condition set* helped build and define the structure as opposed to stripping away existing variables to expose the fundamental system. The process provided insight as to how the fundamental variables develop and how quickly the variable become interdependent on other unconsidered variables.

The *ideal condition set* also highlights that once a system has been fully understood is, it possible to manipulate it. It is possible to alter it and have a basic idea of the resulting outcome after manipulation. In this conceptualization, building upon a misunderstood error is like building upon a crumbling foundation. It demonstrates that most progress in the exploration of new systems is quite slow because the fundamental variables must first be discovered and/or defined. The *ideal condition set* also illustrates that a theory does not always need to be real to be useful. Some sets are purely theoretical postulations that have been proven to be true by current means of understanding (i.e. making an initial belief tangible). It does not necessarily mean that this is the reality, but only that it agrees with established and known perceptions of the real world. Defining an *ideal condition set* may be applied on any level of research and is important in the process of conceptualization. Once these sets are defined it is possible to apply them to similar situations, i.e. a good grounding or blueprint is established, upon which other projects can build.

Throughout the development of the Dod, even though the emphasis is on developing a more suitable and autonomous agent for the programmable/shape-shifting matter domain, a strong underlying philosophical influence on the research is the consideration that artificial intelligence is incomplete without an artificial awareness. Projects that demonstrate robots with capabilities of responding to human conversation (e.g. Turing test) or exhibiting behaviours that can be interpreted by humans as mimicking emotions, suggests that these components are comprised of specific patterns, motions and algorithms [62–64]. These algorithms can be learnt by each system (depending on hardware capacity) but are also formulated from elements beyond text, grammar and content to include movement, sound, visuals, texture, etc. [65]. Children learn through observation, exploration, mimic and experimentation to create biological or organic based algorithms.

The element of awareness is less defined because it requires self-reflection and the ability to become more than the initial input or starting point to eventually formulate concepts and processes independently.

The concept of intelligence is itself an issue of *perspective* and is relative. By comparison, awareness is present at different stages and to varying degrees of self-reflective connectedness. For example, a basic form of awareness is facilitated through sensory modalities, it enables the agent to connect with its environment, without the need for the incoming information to be processed further. This is possible for organic as well as inorganic constructs but would only be considered unidirectional. Awareness combined with intelligence enables more effective and varied interactions to occur between an agent and its environment, i.e. interactions become a bidirectional process. The greater the complexity of a living system, regarding shape and form, number of sensory modalities, the capacity to process information, the greater is the complexity in determining the variables involved in awareness and how they affect it. Awareness is a conglomerate of many different aspects (e.g. time, emotion, logic, reason, knowledge, etc.). One method of training awareness is by making connections between knowledge, experiences and the effect on the agent. This process relies on the ability to alter and be open to varying perspectives.

Enabling an agent to become aware and think for itself is also an aspect that can be disconcerting. It potentially means that an agent is no longer necessarily subject to an external force, in particular when it becomes stronger or more powerful than the initial force controlling it. Alternatively, imbuing technology with the capacity to learn behaviours and self-assemble into specific shapes in order to fulfil predetermined requirements, inevitable leads to the questions in philosophy that provide a moral and ethical compass for people. The desired outcome is to achieve intelligent, shape-shifting MAS interfaces that operate according to a user's wishes. What happens when through the AI algorithms the agents evolve beyond their initial programming? etc. Whilst the aim of this paper is not to discuss the ethics of AI technology, these questions will become more relevant as humans strive to replicate every aspect of themselves artificially.

This process of replication addresses another important issue that emerged with respect to defining the more theoretical guidelines for the design of the Dod: the difference between replication and emulation. The difference between these two terms is subtle but can yield substantially diverse outcomes and the Dod embodies this difference. Replication is the process of reproducing an exact copy of an existing system, artefact or structure whereby reliable repetition is an inherent quality of the process [66, 67]. The action of understanding and learning are rooted in this process and it is vital to complete this phase as thoroughly as possible in order to construct a knowledge foundation [67, 68].

Emulation encompasses the idea of copying or imitating an existing system, artefact or structure, however the important difference is that it also holds scope for surpassing the original design, i.e. it represents the evolution of an idea. Original thought or 'strokes of genius' occur on rare occasions. In most cases ideas and creativity are built upon the experience of previous generations and through an emulative process. For example, in Art, painters like Picasso first painted in the style of the time: Realism (life drawings, still life, etc.). Only after he had mastered this art of drawing, he began defining his own interpretation eventually leading to Cubism. His approach supports the concept that building a good foundation is essential in being able to manipulate the knowledge further. Emulation can be viewed from the perspective of applying the knowledge gained through the replication process. Consider the example of flight: the initial attempts of modelling a direct replication, of a bird's wing onto the human physiology, did not work. As the knowledge of the wing and its relationship to its environment (air) was uncovered, new wing designs began to emerge. The concept of wind moving at different speeds over different surfaces creating lift or drag helped inform a wing design that could be used by humans. Therefore, through emulation humans can fly, but not like birds. The essence of what flight means and how it works has been extracted and the knowledge has been adapted and appropriately altered.

With respect to early agent designs and prototypes in the original PhD study [26], it is evident that some of the shapes and constructs used in earlier prototypes did not function appropriately. Whilst they were replicated directly from their original use, they were taken out of the environment for which they were initially designed for and used for tasks that were outside their scope of adaptability, e.g. the shape of an ant claw used for assembly. This highlights the limitations for direct replication and a reason why it is important to extract the core concept or essence of what is needed to provide the parameters for the design. In the case of the Dod, it should behave in essence like an ant colony but rather than creating loose fitting, undulating shapes (e.g. a raft made of ants), the currently desired result is to generate coherent, ordered, and definitive structures.

6 Conclusion

This paper provides a more detailed insight into the method used to develop the Dod's design. Rather than create another prototype in the domain of shape-shifting technology that cannot be applied beyond the lab environment, the aim of the study was to produce a viable blueprint. This blueprint can act as the basis for developments in the present but also provide a canvas for future adaptations, once applications and materials are better defined. The Dod is a multidisciplinary agent because it was created through a multidisciplinary approach. The essence and influence of each researcher is integrated into their work and even though different disciplines have varying degrees of enabling this integration, it is this adaptability and flexibility that can be the greatest asset to future research. It is difficult to define one specific method when using the STEAM approach, however, therein lies the strength of applying this technique. There is still a need for specialists that develop an expertise in one subject or field, but it has also become evident that there is a need for multidisciplinary specialists that communicate and work in the gaps created by field boundaries. When dealing with complex design projects, where there are significant number of unknown variables, it may be worthwhile considering looking at the problem from a different direction, as suggested by the title of this paper.

Acknowledgements. I would like to thank my supervisor Dr. Mikael Fernström, for his guidance throughout my study and for my family for their continued support. Thanks also go to the Irish Research Council for funding the first 3 years of this study (Project ID: GOIPG/2013/351).

References

1. Carroll, L.: Through the Looking Glass. Pan Macmillan, London (1972)
2. Hasenfuss, H.: Reinventing the cube: an alternative agent design for shape-shifting technology. In: Proceedings of the 3rd International Conference on Computer-Human Interaction Research and Applications - Volume 1: CHIRA, ISBN 978-989-758-376-6, ISSN 2184-3244, pp. 15–27 (2019). https://doi.org/10.5220/0008116500150027
3. Follmer, S., et al.: deForm: an interactive malleable surface for capturing 2.5D arbitrary objects, tools and touch. In: Proceedings of the 24th Annual ACM Symposium on User Interface Software and Technology, pp. 527–536. ACM, Santa Barbara, California, USA (2011)
4. Follmer, S., et al.: Jamming user interfaces: programmable particle stiffness and sensing for malleable and shape-changing devices. In: Proceedings of the 25th Annual ACM Symposium on User Interface Software and Technology, ACM, Cambridge, Massachusetts, USA (2012)
5. Follmer, S., et al.: inFORM: dynamic physical affordances and constraints through shape and object actuation, p. 10. ACM (2013)
6. Coelho, M., Ishii, H., Maes, P.: Surflex: a programmable surface for the design of tangible interfaces. In: CHI, Human Factors in Computing Systems. Florenece, Italy, pp. 3429–3434 (2008)
7. Coelho, M., Maes, P.: Sprout I/O: a texturally rich interface. In: Proceedings of the 2nd International Conference on Tangible and Embedded Interaction, pp. 221–222. ACM, Bonn, Germany (2008)
8. Ishii, H., Ullmer, B.: Tangible bits: towards seamless interfaces between people, bits and atoms. In: Proceedings of the ACM SIGCHI Conference on Human Factors in Computing Systems, pp. 234–241. ACM, Atlanta, Georgia, USA (1997)
9. Minuto, A., Huisman, G., Nijholt, A.: Follow the grass: a smart material interactive pervasive display. In: Herrlich, M., Malaka, R., Masuch, M. (eds.) ICEC 2012. LNCS, vol. 7522, pp. 144–157. Springer, Heidelberg (2012). https://doi.org/10.1007/978-3-642-33542-6_13
10. Rozin, D.: Pom Pom Mirror. Bitforms Gallery, NYC (2015)
11. Grünwald, M.: Human Haptic Perception: Basics and Applications. Birkhäuser, Basel (2008)
12. Kern, T.A.: Engineering Haptic Devices. Springer-Verlag, Heidelberg (2009)
13. MacLean, K.E.: Haptic interaction design for everyday interfaces. Hum. Factors Ergon. Soc. 4(1), 149–194 (2008)
14. Saddik, A.E., et al.: Haptics Technologies, in Bringing Touch to Multimedia, Springer Berlin, Heidelberg (2011)
15. Parkes, A., Ishii, H.: Bosu: a physical programmable design tool for transformability with soft mechanics. In: Proceedings of the 8th ACM Conference on Designing Interactive Systems, pp. 189–198. ACM, Aarhus, Denmark (2010)
16. Rasmussen, M.K., et al.: Shape-changing interfaces: a review of the design space and open research questions. In: CHI, Hot Moves: Shape-Changing & Thermal Interfaces, Austin, Texas, USA, pp. 735–744 (2012)
17. Tactus Technology: Taking touch screen interfaces into a new dimension. In: Tactus Technology, p. 13 (2012)
18. Hook, J., et al.: A reconfigurable ferromagnetic input device. In: Proceedings of the 22nd Annual ACM Symposium on User Interface Software and Technology, pp. 51–54. ACM, Victoria, BC, Canada (2009)
19. Vousden, M.: What is VW BlueMotion. 2015 18 October 2016. https://www.carwow.co.uk/blog/volkswagen-bluemotion-explained
20. Nakagawa, Y., Kamimura, A., Kawaguchi, Y.: MimicTile: a variable stiffness deformable user interface for mobile devices. In: CHI, Hot Moves: Shape-changing & Thermal Interfaces, Austin, Texas, USA, pp. 745–748 (2012)

21. Taylor, B.T., Bove Jr, M.V.: Graspables: grasp-recognition as a user interface. In: Proceedings of the SIGCHI Conference on Human Factors in Computing Systems, pp. 917–926. ACM, Boston, MA, USA (2009)

22. Horev, O.: Talking to the hand. An exploration into shape shifting objects and morphing interfaces. Interaction Design Institute Ivrea (2006)

23. Michelitsch, G., et al.: Haptic chameleon: a new concept of shape-changing user interface controls with force feedback. In: Extended Abstracts on Human Factors in Computing Systems (2004)

24. Parkes, A., Poupyrev, I., Ishii, H.: Designing kinetic interactions for organic user interfaces. Commun. ACM **51**(6), 58–65 (2008)

25. Monnai, Y., et al.: HaptoMime: mid-air haptic interaction with a floating virtual screen. In: Proceedings of the 27th Annual ACM Symposium on User Interface Software and Technology, pp. 663–667. ACM, Honolulu, Hawaii, USA (2014)

26. Hasenfuss, H.: A design exploration of an agent template for multiagent systems (MAS) for shape shifting tangible user interfaces. In: Computer Science and Information Systems, University of Limerick (2018)

27. Weiser, M.: The computer for the 21st century. Scientific American Ubicomp (1991)

28. Gorbet, M.G., Orth, M., Ishii, H.: Triangles: tangible interface for manipulation and exploration of digital information topography. In: Proceedings of the SIGCHI Conference on Human Factors in Computing Systems, pp. 49–56. ACM Press/Addison-Wesley Publishing Co.: Los Angeles, California, USA (1998)

29. Kim, H., Lee, W.: Kinetic tiles: modular construction units for interactive kinetic surfaces. In: Adjunct Proceedings of the 23nd Annual ACM Symposium on User Interface Software and Technology, pp. 431–432. ACM, New York, USA (2010)

30. Lifton, J.H., Broxton, M., Paradiso, J.A.: Distributed sensor networks as sensate skin. BT Technol. J. **22**(4), 32–44 (2004)

31. Patten, J., et al.: Sensetable: a wireless object tracking platform for tangible user interfaces. In: Proceedings of the SIGCHI Conference on Human Factors in Computing Systems, pp. 253–260. ACM, Seattle, Washington, USA (2001)

32. Rekimoto, J.: SmartSkin: an infrastructure for freehand manipulation on interactive surfaces. In: Proceedings of the SIGCHI Conference on Human Factors in Computing Systems, pp. 113–120. ACM, Minneapolis, Minnesota, USA (2002)

33. McElligott, L., Dillon, M., Leydon, K., Richardson, B., Fernström, M., Paradiso, J.A.: 'ForSe FIELds' - force sensors for interactive environments. In: Borriello, G., Holmquist, L.E. (eds.) UbiComp 2002. LNCS, vol. 2498, pp. 168–175. Springer, Heidelberg (2002). https://doi.org/10.1007/3-540-45809-3_13

34. Le Goc, M., et al.: Zooids: building blocks for swarm user interfaces. In: Proceedings of the Symposion on User Interface Software and Technology (UIST). New York (2016)

35. Rubenstein, M., Cornejo, A., Nagpal, R.: Programmable self-assembly in a thousand-robot swarm. Science **345**(6198), 795 (2014)

36. Whitesides, G.M., Grzybowski, B.: Self-assembly at all scales. Science **295**(5564), 2418–2421 (2002)

37. Mlot, N.J., Tovey, C.A., Hu, D.L.: Fire ants self-assemble into waterproof rafts to survive floods. Proc. Natl. Acad. Sci. U. S. Am. **108**(19), 7669–7673 (2011)

38. Dumpert, K.: The Social Biology of Ants. The Pitman Press, Bath (1978)

39. Gordon, D.M., Colonial Studies. Boston Review, pp. 59–62 (2010)

40. Bergbreiter, S.: Why I make robots the size of a grain of rice. TED Talks 2014 7 September 2015. https://www.ted.com/talks/sarah_bergbreiter_why_i_make_robots_the_size_of_a_grain_of_rice?language=en

41. Christensen, D.L., et al.: μTugs: enabling microrobots to deliver macro forces with controllable adhesives. In: 2015 IEEE International Conference on Robotics and Automation (ICRA) (2015)

42. Kasade, N.: A ball of fire ants behaves like a material. Youtube (2014)

43. Bay, M.: Transformers: Revenge of the Fallen. Dreamworks, Paramount Pictures, California (2009)

44. Cameron, J.: Terminator 2. Carolco Pictures, Pacific Western, Boca Raton (1991)

45. Lin, J.: Star Trek: Beyond. Paramount Pictures, Skydance Media, Santa Monica (2016)

46. Mangold, J.: The Wolverine. Twentieth Century Fox (2013)

47. Taylor, A.: Terminator Genisys. Paramount Pictures, Skydance Media (2015)

48. Hannula, M.: Catch me if you can: chances and challenges of artistic research. Art and Research **2**(2) (2009)

49. Caduff, C.: Artistic research: methods -development of a discourse - current risks, pp. 310–323 (2011)

50. Cheng, N.G., et al.: Thermally tunable, self-healing composites for soft robotic applications. Macromol. Mater. Eng. **299**(11), 1279–1284 (2014)

51. Lv, C., et al.: Origami based mechanical metamaterials. Sci. Rep. **4**, 5979 (2014)

52. Overvelde, J.T.B., et al.: A three-dimensional actuated origami-inspired transformable metamaterial with multiple degrees of freedom. Nat. Commun. **7**, 10929 (2016)

53. Reis, P.M., López Jiménez, F., Marthelot, J.: Transforming architectures inspired by origami. Proc. Natl. Acad. Sci. U. S. Am. **112**(40), 12234–12235 (2015)

54. Silverberg, J.L., et al.: Using origami design principles to fold reprogrammable mechanical metamaterials. Science **345**(6197), 647 (2014)

55. Ausareny, J., et al.: Open source hardware (OSHW) supporting interaction between traditional crafts and emergent science: wayang kulit over microfluidic interfaces. In: SIGGRAPH Asia 2014 Designing Tools For Crafting Interactive Artifacts, pp. 1–4. ACM, Shenzhen, China (2014)

56. British Council.: FameLab Ireland. 2015 Oct 2015. https://www.britishcouncil.ie/famelab

57. Meyer, V.: Merging science and art through fungi. Fungal Biol. Biotechnol. **6**(1), 5 (2019)

58. Eichenlaub, M.: What did Richard Feynman mean when he said, "What I cannot create, I do not understand"? 2015 4 January 2015 13 June 2016. https://www.quora.com/What-did-Richard-Feynman-mean-when-he-said-What-I-cannot-create-I-do-not-understand

59. Hofstadter, D.R.: Fluid concepts and creative analogies: computer models of the fundamental mechanisms of thought. 1945-; Fluid Analogies Research Group, Allen Lane the Penguin Press, London (1995)

60. Sieden, L.S.: Buckminster Fuller's Universe: His Life and Work. Mass: Perseus, Cambridge (1989)

61. Durst, F.: Fluid Mechanics: An Introduction to the Theory of Fluid Flows. Springer, Berlin Heidelberg (2008)

62. Nakayasu, A.: Himawari: shape memory alloy motion display for robotic representation. In: CHI, Human Factors in Computing Systems, Atlanta, GA, USA, pp. 4327–4332 (2010)

63. Togler, J., Hemmert, F., Wettach, R.: Living interfaces: the thrifty faucet. In: Proceedings of the 3rd International Conference on Tangible and Embedded Interaction, pp. 43–44. ACM, Cambridge, United Kingdom (2009)

64. Wakita, A., Shibutani, M., Tsuji, K.: Emotional smart materials. In: Jacko, J.A. (ed.) HCI 2009. LNCS, vol. 5612, pp. 802–805. Springer, Heidelberg (2009). https://doi.org/10.1007/978-3-642-02580-8_88

65. Clemenger, S.: Bio-likeness: Getting the feel of our robotic future. 2014 7 July 2015. http://www.gizmag.com/bio-likeness-yamanka-robots/32836/

66. Festo: Find out how Industry 4.0 can reach the next level. 2018 Feb 2018. https://www.festo.com/group/en/cms/11753.htm

67. Ridden, P.: Festo unveils robotic ants, butterflies and chameleon tongue gripper. Gizmag 2015 14 June 2016. http://www.gizmag.com/festo-bionicants-flexshapegripper-emotionbutterflies/36765/
68. Robugtix: T8X - Looks like a spider. Moves like a spider. 2013 14 June 2016. http://www.robugtix.com/t8x/

Randomised Controlled Cross-Over Trial Measuring Brain-Computer Interface Metrics to Characterise the User Experience of Search Engines When Ambiguous Search Queries Are Used

Wynand Nel[1]([✉]) [iD], Lizette De Wet[1] [iD], and Robert Schall[2] [iD]

[1] Department of Computer Science and Informatics, University of the Free State, Nelson Mandela Drive, Bloemfontein, South Africa
{nelw,dwetl}@ufs.ac.za
[2] Department of Mathematical Statistics and Actuarial Science, University of the Free State, Nelson Mandela Drive, Bloemfontein, South Africa
schallr@ufs.ac.za

Abstract. Retrieving information through World Wide Web searches is part of daily life. Many people prefer using short search strings/queries which can be ambiguous because of their brevity. This ambiguity often causes search engines to return thousands of irrelevant results which can cause frustration with the particular search engine. Consequently, users might rate the particular search engine unfavourably. We conducted a randomised controlled cross-over trial with a Graeco-Latin Square design to measure various user emotions (Frustration, Excitement, Meditation and Engagement) with a Brain-Computer Interface while participants performed ambiguous Internet searches in Google, Yahoo! and Bing. The study results suggest that emotion data captured with a Brain-Computer Interface together with the pre-test and post-test questionnaire feedback can be used to characterise the user experience of different search engines when searches are conducted using ambiguous search terms. In particular, the effect of Search Engine and Search Term had a significant outcome on the measured emotions, while the effect of Occasion was not significant.

Keywords: Ambiguous search queries · Brain-Computer Interface · Emotions · Engagement · Frustration · Information retrieval · Long-Term Excitement · Meditation · Search engine · Short-Term Excitement · User experience

1 Introduction

Computers form an integral part of our lives today, thus the reference to the digital age. Searching for information is a day-to-day task for many people. These searches can be conducted using the non-electronic sources, such as printed material, or they can take the form of electronic/digital searches of the World Wide Web (WWW). The WWW is used by many as their primary source of information.

© Springer Nature Switzerland AG 2021
M. J. Escalona et al. (Eds.): CHIRA 2018/CHIRA 2019, CCIS 1351, pp. 102–123, 2021.
https://doi.org/10.1007/978-3-030-67108-2_6

It is, therefore, imperative that researchers/technology practitioners study the use of technology-based products and their effect on User Experience (UX) and usability. To investigate the UX of participants when performing these electronic searches, especially when performing ambiguous search queries, we conducted a randomised controlled trial measuring Brain-Computer Interface (BCI) metrics to characterise the UX of three Search Engines, namely Google, Yahoo! and Bing, when ambiguous queries are used.

2   Background

The WWW consists of trillions of web pages and grows by several million pages per day as more information is added [2, 28]. The objective of a website is to share information, but Information Retrieval (IR) is challenged by the daily addition of millions of pages to the WWW [11].

IR is defined as an information-seeking activity that supports people's interaction with the text [4]; information retrieval falls in the sub-field of computer science that deals with the automated storage and retrieval of documents [15]. Referring to Fig. 1, the user's information need is driven by a task. This need is verbalised (usually mentally) and translated into a search query that is submitted to a system, which in turn, searches through a collection of documents returning some results. Users, upon inspecting the returned results, can then refine the search query in order to refine the search results [7].

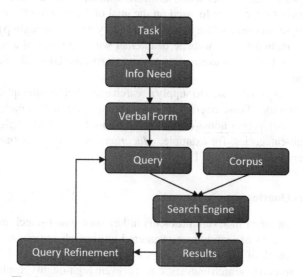

Fig. 1. The classic model for IR, augmented for the web [7].

For a user to find specific information on the WWW, he/she needs to know the address (Uniform Resource Locator - URL) of that information. The problem originates from the fact that this URL is seldom available to the user beforehand. Thus, utilising search engines has become the only practical method to find information on the WWW

[17]. This fact resulted in search engines becoming the most accessed web sites on the Internet [11, 28].

Search engines are web-based systems for finding distributed data on the Internet and organising it into logical searchable databases by using keywords [6, 52, 53]. Many search engines are available, each having their specific features, for example, their unique algorithms that result in the returning of unique result sets [28, 30].

Some search engines are very comprehensive and can include thousands of results in their result set, depending on the executed search query. Research has shown that users prefer short search queries which could cause ambiguity within the search engine returning more results than needed [40]. For example, the word "canon" as a search query, could imply an interest in the latest DSLR Canon camera, but the returned results may instead provide information on the Japanese multinational corporation.

The disadvantage of short, ambiguous queries is that the users need to work through many irrelevant results in search of the required resource. When asked to do so, a user might rate their experience (UX) with the search engine's handling of ambiguous queries, unfavourably (when only traditional UX measurements, like questionnaires or interviews, are used).

3   Search Queries

Internet search queries can be categorised as informational, transactional or navigational [7, 32]. Informational queries are focused on the goal of the user to obtain information about a specific topic, whereas, with a transactional query, a user would shop for a product or download information from a website or interact with the result of a website. With navigational queries, the goal is to navigate a user to a specific URL, like the homepage of an organisation.

Search engines rely on the users to supply a search query before attempting to retrieve the relevant information. These queries can be clear (specific, with a narrow topic, for example, *Windows 10*); proper nouns (names or locations, for example, *Jefferson*); broad (having many sub-categories, for example, *education*); or ambiguous (more than one meaning, for example, *seal*) [3, 10, 12, 33, 37].

3.1   Ambiguous Queries

Word ambiguity can result in severe problems in keyword-based search methods [48]. Approximately 7%–23% of search queries entered into search engines are ambiguous, with the average length of these search queries being one word [33, 36]. Short search queries, when submitted to search engines, could prevent high-quality results, the reason being that not enough/clear information is presented to the ranking algorithm of the search engine, causing it to return a diverse set of results [23].

The word *ruby* is an example of an ambiguous search query. What does a person expect the search engine to return when the word *ruby* is entered as a search query? Is the person searching for the Ruby computer programming language or rather information about the gemstone? If the person is indeed searching for the gemstone, what specifically is he/she searching for? General information on the gemstone or maybe where to buy it?

4   User Experience (UX)

UX is defined as a broad view on every aspect of the interaction or anticipated interaction [20] that a user has with a company, its services and products, taking into account the feelings, perceptions and thoughts of the user [27, 43, 44] (Fig. 2).

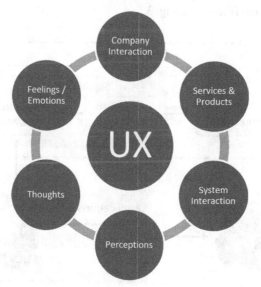

Fig. 2. Definition of UX [Adapted from 20, 28, 44, 45].

The evolution of technology does not necessarily mean that technologies are becoming easier to use, and as such, UX must be given attention and importance [43]. UX is specifically about how people feel about the product, their satisfaction and pleasure when using it, opening it or looking at it [29, 31]. This includes the user's overall impression of how good (or bad) the product is to use, down to the smallest detail.

Many aspects characterise UX, including usability, functionality, aesthetics, content, look and feel, and the sensual and emotional feel are all of central importance [29]. McCarthy and Wright [24] highlight the importance of people's expectations when characterising UX and how they make sense of their experiences when using technology. Their framework, Technology as Experience, explains UX largely in terms of how it is felt by the user. Some other aspects of UX include fun, health, social capital (the social resources that are maintained through shared values, norms, social networks and goals) and cultural identity (race, age, ethnicity, disability, etcetera) [8].

5   Bain-Computer Interface (BCI)

Brain-Computer Interaction transforms intentions into operational commands through a functional interface without any motor action. Thus, a BCI enables individuals to control external devices like a computer [5, 19, 35, 45]. A BCI can be defined as a communication system where the messages sent by a person to the external world does not pass through the brain's normal output pathways of nerves and muscles (e.g. speech and gestures) [46]. Instead, a BCI harnesses bio-potentials, namely electric signals originating from the brain and nervous system [9] which are under the conscious control of the user [46]. The BCI measures Electroencephalography (EEG) signals on the outside of the skull before decoding them into computer-understood commands [9, 26, 41, 46]. A basic design of a BCI system is shown in Fig. 3.

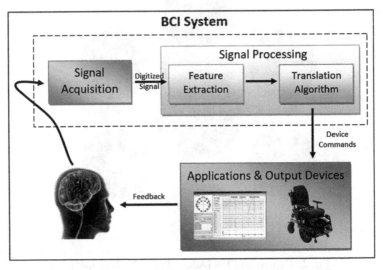

Fig. 3. Basic design of a BCI system [Adapted from 41, 46].

A BCI can be classified as either being invasive or non-invasive. Invasive BCIs record the signal from within the brain, whereas a non-invasive BCI (like EEG) acquire the signal from the scalp [21, 26, 35, 46]. This study made use of a non-invasive BCI device as it was a low-cost method without posing any risk to the participant [35].

Non-invasive BCI devices can measure different bio-potentials, including EEG, MEG (Magnetoencephalography), fMRI (Functional Magnetic Resonance Imaging), EMG (Electromyography) and NIRS (Near Infrared Spectroscopy). This study measured EEG signals, with it being the most widely used low-cost, low-risk neuroimaging method with high portability and high temporal resolution [26, 38, 45].

5.1 Measuring Emotions

Although it is difficult to measure emotions [43] and because there are no internationally recognised units for measuring emotions [16, 47], understanding the emotional state of a participant is important to the UX researcher. Emotions are often hidden, fleeting or conflicted, and participants might tell the researcher what they think he/she wants to hear. Alternatively, they might find it difficult to articulate how they feel when asked. Some participants might not feel comfortable admitting to what they feel to a complete stranger [34, 43].

An emotion can be divided into arousal and valence. During the arousal (stress) state, a person's emotions can range between calm and excited, whereas a person's emotions vary between positive and negative during the valence (affect) state [1] (Fig. 4).

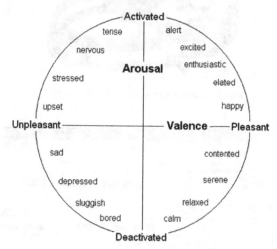

Fig. 4. Two-dimensional representation of emotional state, governed by valence and arousal [42].

User emotions can also be measured [1, 34, 43] based on the facial expressions of a user; observing the behaviours of a user; measuring the heart rate and stress levels; recording a person's pupil diameter [18] and blink rates [39]; measuring the skin conductance of a user, and translating EEG measurements into user emotions.

5.2 Emotiv EPOC Neuroheadset

This study made use of the Emotiv EPOC Neuroheadset (Fig. 5), developed by Emotiv (a neuro-engineering company). The Emotiv is a high-fidelity, high-resolution 14-channel wireless neuroheadset designed for human-computer interaction. The Emotiv headset can detect user-trained mental commands, subconscious emotional states and facial expressions which allow the computer to react to a user's moods and deliberate commands in a more natural way [13, 14].

The Emotiv allows for EEG observations through its detection suites (Affectiv^{TM}, Cognitiv^{TM} and Expressiv^{TM}) which are based on the combined pattern of neuron activity of different regions of the brain. Each individual sensor is updated twice per second with very detailed information accessible through the provided Software Development Kit (SDK) [50].

The Affectiv^{TM} suite (Fig. 6) was deemed most appropriate for this research, as it could detect a participants' engagement, frustration, excitement, boredom, and meditation levels in real-time. A detailed explanation of the individual emotions was given in a previous paper [25].

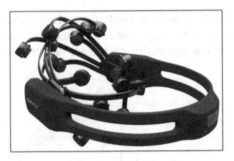

Fig. 5. Emotiv EPOC neuroheadset [13].

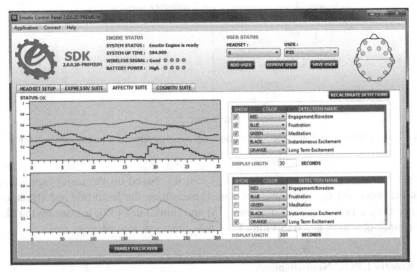

Fig. 6. The Affectiv™ suite of the emotiv control panel [25].

6 Methodology

The primary goal of this study was to characterise by means of BCI measurements the UX of different search engines when participants performed searches that involved ambiguous search queries. In order to achieve this goal, the following research question was formulated:

What are the effects of Search Engine, Search Term and Occasion on the BCI Metrics (Minimum, Maximum, Average and Fluctuation) for the different emotions (Long-Term Excitement, Short-Term Excitement, Engagement, Meditation and Frustration)?

6.1 Testing Procedure

A total of 36 participants (19 males and 17 females; age range 18–26 years) were recruited. All participants were first-year students at the University of the Free State (UFS) enrolled in the computer literacy course.

As part of the testing procedure, each participant had to complete a pre-test questionnaire, conduct three ambiguous search engine searches and complete a post-test questionnaire. The Emotiv EPOC Neuroheadset was fitted and allowed time to stabilise the brainwave detections while the participants completed the pre-test questionnaire [25]. The questionnaire collected personal information, as well as the participants' experience with computers, the WWW, performing searches and search-engines. Based on this information, the participants' self-rated technological experience was calculated as Expert Frequent Users.

6.2 Tasks

The trial's cross-over design required participants to carry out three WWW searches on three occasions, using combinations of three search engines (Google, Yahoo! and Bing) and three ambiguous search terms (Shoot, Divide and Seal). Participants were randomised to the nine unique search engine/search term combinations using a Graeco-Latin Square design [22]. This design allowed for the statistically efficient assessment of the effects of Search Engine, Search Term, and Occasion.

The three search terms were chosen from a list of 27 ambiguous search terms, all exhibiting the same characteristics across Google, Yahoo! and Bing [25]. Since the users were not allowed to use the keyboard to change the search string, it was crucial that the "Searches related to [original search string]" in Google [51], "Also Try" in Yahoo! [54], and "Related searches" in Bing [49], displayed the same results once the search was completed. The specific search engine suggestions (above) are displayed to assist users in formulating (through selection) more relevant search queries. Google, Yahoo! and Bing display these suggestions towards the bottom of the web page, with Bing also displaying them at the top right.

The participants wore the BCI headset while completing the search tasks. The BCI headset recorded the participants' emotional data (in real-time) while they were completing each task. The recorded emotional data included Long-Term and Short-Term Excitement, Engagement, Meditation and Frustration. The data from the individual profiles, recorded over time, were cleaned and normalised before four summary metrics were calculated per emotion. These metrics were:

- Minimum (Min): Minimum value measured during the recording period.
- Maximum (Max): Maximum value measured during the recording period.
- Average (Avg): Arithmetic mean of all values measured during the recording period.
- Fluctuation: Calculated as the normalised peak-trough fluctuation, namely (max−min)/average.

7 Statistical Analysis

The following null hypotheses were formulated in order to statistically assess the effect of Search Engine, Search Term and Occasion on the BCI metrics calculated from five emotions:

$H_{0,1}$: *There are no differences between the mean BCI metrics (Minimum, Maximum, Average and Fluctuation) calculated for the different emotions (Long-Term Excitement, Short-Term Excitement, Engagement, Meditation and Frustration) with regard to the factors Search Engine (Google, Yahoo! and Bing), Search Term (Shoot, Divide and Seal) and Occasion (First, Second and Third).*

Sixty hypotheses were tested (5 emotions each with 4 metrics and 3 factors; $5 \times 4 \times 3 = 60$).

The four summary metrics of the BCI data (Minimum, Maximum, Average and Fluctuation) for each emotion (Long-Term Excitement, Short-Term Excitement, Engagement, Meditation and Frustration), were analysed using ANOVA fitting the factors Participant, Occasion, Search Term and Search Engine. From this ANOVA, F-statistics and P-values associated with the factors Occasion, Search Term and Search Engine were calculated. Furthermore, mean values of each metric and emotion, for each level of the factors, Occasion, Search Term and Search Engine, were reported.

With regard to each metric and emotion, the three search engines were compared by calculating point estimates for the pairwise differences in mean values between search engines, as well as 95% confidence intervals for the mean difference and the associated P-values. Search terms and occasions were compared similarly.

7.1 Long-Term Excitement

The mean values and overall F-test for the effects of Search Engine, Search Term and Occasion on the BCI metrics, for the emotion Long-Term Excitement will be discussed below.

Effect of Search Engine. The mean values and overall F-test for the effect of *Search Engine* on BCI metrics for the emotion *Long-Term Excitement* are displayed in Table 1.

For the emotion Long-Term Excitement, the Minimum metric showed statistically significant differences between search engines (P = 0.0075), with Google having the greatest mean minimum (0.29), followed by Bing (0.24) and Yahoo! (0.20). In contrast, the Maximum and Average metrics did not show statistically significant differences. The Fluctuation metric showed statistically significant differences between search engines (P = 0.0053) with Google showing the lowest mean fluctuation (0.87), followed by Bing (1.00) and Yahoo! (1.27). The fact that Yahoo! had the greatest mean Fluctuation metric can probably be explained by the fact that this search engine had the smallest mean Minimum metric, while the mean Maximum and mean Average metrics did not differ significantly between search engines.

Effect of Search Term. The mean values and overall F-test for the effect of *Search Term* on BCI metrics for the emotion *Long-Term Excitement* are displayed in Table 2.

Table 1. Effect of search engine on BCI metrics for the emotion *Long-Term Excitement*: mean values and overall F-test.

Emotion	Metric	Search engine	Mean	F-statistic[a]	P-value[a]
Long-Term Excitement	Min	Bing	0.24	5.27	0.0075
		Google	0.29		
		Yahoo!	0.20		
	Max	Bing	0.64	0.05	0.9526
		Google	0.64		
		Yahoo!	0.65		
	Avg	Bing	0.43	2.22	0.1164
		Google	0.46		
		Yahoo!	0.40		
	Fluctuation	Bing	1.00	5.69	0.0053
		Google	0.87		
		Yahoo!	1.27		

[a]F-test for null-hypothesis of no effect of *Search Engine*, from ANOVA with *Participant*, *Search Engine*, *Search Term* and *Occasion* as fixed effects; F-statistic has 2 and 66 degrees of freedom. Significant P-values ($P < 0.05$) are underlined.

Table 2. Effect of search term on BCI metrics for the Emotion *Long-Term Excitement*: mean values and overall F-test.

Emotion	Metric	Search term	Mean	F-statistic[a]	P-value[a]
Lon-Term Excitement	Min	Shoot	0.26	6.13	0.0036
		Divide	0.19		
		Seal	0.28		
	Max	Shoot	0.61	2.86	0.0643
		Divide	0.69		
		Seal	0.64		
	Avg	Shoot	0.43	0.76	0.4707
		Divide	0.40		
		Seal	0.45		
	Fluctuation	Shoot	0.88	7.99	0.0008
		Divide	1.32		
		Seal	0.94		

[a]F-test for null-hypothesis of no effect of *Search Term*, from ANOVA with *Participant*, *Search Engine*, *Search Term* and *Occasion* as fixed effects; F-statistic has 2 and 66 degrees of freedom. Significant P-values ($P < 0.05$) are underlined.

Regarding Long-Term Excitement, the Minimum metric showed statistically significant differences between search terms ($P = 0.0036$), with Seal having the greatest mean minimum (0.28), followed by Shoot (0.26) and Divide (0.19). The Maximum and Average metrics did not show statistically significant differences. The Fluctuation metric showed statistically significant differences between search terms (P = 0.0008) with Shoot showing the lowest mean Fluctuation (0.88) followed by Seal (0.94) and Divide (1.32). The fact that Divide had the greatest mean Fluctuation metric can probably be explained by the fact that this Search Term had the smallest mean Minimum metric, while the mean Maximum and mean Average metrics did not differ significantly between Search Terms.

Effect of Occasion. Regarding Long-Term Excitement, none of the metrics showed statistically significant differences between occasions.

7.2 Short-Term Excitement

Effect of Search Engine. The mean values and overall F-test for the effect of *Search Engine* on BCI metrics for the emotion *Short-Term Excitement* are displayed in Table 3.

Table 3. Effect of search engine on BCI metrics for the emotion *Short-Term Excitement*: mean values and overall F-test.

Emotion	Metric	Search Engine	Mean	F-statistic[a]	P-value[a]
Short-Term Excitement	Min	Bing	0.05	7.38	<u>0.0013</u>
		Google	0.10		
		Yahoo!	0.04		
	Max	Bing	0.90	1.57	0.215
		Google	0.91		
		Yahoo!	0.95		
	Avg	Bing	0.43	1.51	0.2278
		Google	0.45		
		Yahoo!	0.40		
	Fluctuation	Bing	2.15	5.46	<u>0.0064</u>
		Google	2.10		
		Yahoo!	2.53		

[a]F-test for null-hypothesis of no effect of *Search Engine*, from ANOVA with *Participant*, *Search Engine*, *Search Term* and *Occasion* as fixed effects; F-statistic has 2 and 66 degrees of freedom. Significant P-values (P < 0.05) are underlined.

For the emotion Short-Term Excitement, the Minimum metric showed statistically significant differences between search engines (P = 0.0013), with Google having the greatest mean minimum (0.10) followed by Bing (0.05) and Yahoo! (0.04). In contrast, the Maximum and Average metrics did not show statistically significant differences. The

Fluctuation metric showed statistically significant differences between search engines (P = 0.0064), with Google showing the lowest mean fluctuation (2.10) followed by Bing (2.15) and Yahoo! (2.53). The fact that Yahoo! had the greatest mean Fluctuation metric can probably be explained by the fact that this search engine had the smallest mean Minimum metric, while the mean Maximum and mean Average metrics did not differ significantly between search engines.

Effect of Search Term. The mean values and overall F-test for the effect of *Search Term* on BCI metrics for the emotion *Short-Term Excitement* are displayed in Table 4.

Table 4. Effect of search term on BCI metrics for the emotion *Short-Term Excitement*: mean values and overall F-test.

Emotion	Metric	Search term	Mean	F-statistic[a]	P-value[a]
Short-Term Excitement	Min	Shoot	0.07	3.33	0.0418
		Divide	0.04		
		Seal	0.08		
	Max	Shoot	0.90	3.02	0.0556
		Divide	0.96		
		Seal	0.90		
	Avg	Shoot	0.43	0.75	0.4771
		Divide	0.41		
		Seal	0.44		
	Fluctuation	Shoot	2.20	3.14	0.0496
		Divide	2.46		
		Seal	2.12		

[a]F-test for null-hypothesis of no effect of *Search Term*, from ANOVA with *Participant, Search Engine, Search Term* and *Occasion* as fixed effects; F-statistic has 2 and 66 degrees of freedom. Significant P-values (P < 0.05) are underlined.

For the emotion Short-Term Excitement, the Minimum metric showed statistically significant differences between search terms (P = 0.0418), with Seal having the greatest mean minimum (0.08) followed by Shoot (0.07) and Divide (0.04). In contrast, the Maximum and Average metrics did not show statistically significant differences. The Fluctuation metric showed statistically significant differences between search engines (P = 0.0496) with Seal showing the lowest mean fluctuation (2.12), followed by Shoot (2.20) and Divide (2.46). The fact that Divide had the greatest mean Fluctuation metric can probably be explained by the fact that this search term had the smallest mean Minimum metric, while the mean Maximum and mean Average metrics did not differ significantly between search terms.

Effect of Occasion. Regarding Short-Term Excitement, none of the metrics Minimum, Maximum, Average and Fluctuation, showed statistically significant differences between occasions.

7.3 Engagement

Effect of Search Engine. For the emotion Engagement, none of the metrics showed statistically significant differences between search engines, indicating that this BCI emotion does not discriminate between the three search engines.

Effect of Search Term. The mean values and overall F-test for the effect of *Search Term* on BCI metrics for the emotion *Engagement* are displayed in Table 5.

Table 5. Effect of search term on BCI metrics for the emotion *Engagement*: mean values and overall F-test.

Emotion	Metric	Search term	Mean	F-statistic[a]	P-value[a]
Engagement	Min	Shoot	0.46	8.78	0.0004
		Divide	0.40		
		Seal	0.46		
	Max	Shoot	0.77	6.57	0.0025
		Divide	0.83		
		Seal	0.78		
	Avg	Shoot	0.59	0.99	0.3784
		Divide	0.59		
		Seal	0.60		
	Fluctuation	Shoot	0.52	16.3	<.0001
		Divide	0.74		
		Seal	0.55		

[a]F-test for null-hypothesis of no effect of *Search Term*, from ANOVA with *Participant*, *Search Engine*, *Search Term* and *Occasion* as fixed effects; F-statistic has 2 and 66 degrees of freedom. Significant P-values ($P < 0.05$) are underlined.

For the emotion Engagement, the Minimum metric showed statistically significant differences between search terms ($P = 0.0004$), with Seal and Shoot having the greatest mean minimum (0.46) followed by Divide (0.40). The Maximum metric also indicated statistically significant differences between the search terms ($P = 0.0025$). Shoot has the lowest mean maximum (0.77), followed by Seal (0.78) and Divide (0.83). The Average metric is the only metric not showing statistically significant differences. The Fluctuation metric showed statistically significant differences between search engines ($P < 0.0001$) with Shoot showing the lowest mean fluctuation (0.52) followed by Seal (0.55) and Divide (0.74). The fact that Divide had the greatest mean Fluctuation metric can probably be explained by the fact that this search term had the smallest mean Minimum and highest mean Maximum metric. This search term was also the only search term that required the participant to view three web pages before finding the correct answer. The findings of the SUS scores indicated that the participants experienced the task, using the search term Divide, to be more difficult than terms Shoot and Seal.

Effect of Occasion. The mean values and overall F-test for the effect of *Occasion* on BCI metrics for the emotion *Engagement* are displayed in Table 6.

Table 6. Effect of occasion on BCI metrics for the emotion *Engagement*: mean values and overall F-test.

Emotion	Metric	Occasion	Mean	F-statistic[a]	P-value[a]
Engagement	Min	First	0.44	0.34	0.7125
		Second	0.44		
		Third	0.43		
	Max	First	0.81	1.7	0.1904
		Second	0.77		
		Third	0.79		
	Avg	First	0.61	4.3	0.0176
		Second	0.59		
		Third	0.58		
	Fluctuation	First	0.61	0.54	0.5881
		Second	0.58		
		Third	0.62		

[a]F-test for null-hypothesis of no effect of *Occasion*, from ANOVA with *Participant*, *Search Engine*, *Search Term* and *Occasion* as fixed effects; F-statistic has 2 and 66 degrees of freedom. Significant P-values ($P < 0.05$) are underlined.

For the emotion Engagement, the metrics Minimum, Maximum and Fluctuation did not show any statistically significant differences between occasions. The Average metric showed statistically significant differences ($P = 0.0176$), with the Second Occasion having the lowest average mean (0.58), followed by the First (0.61) and Third Occasions (0.62).

7.4 Meditation

Effect of Search Engine. The mean values and overall F-test for the effect of *Search Engine* on BCI metrics for the emotion *Meditation* are displayed in Table 7.

Table 7. Effect of search engine on BCI metrics for the emotion *Meditation*: mean values and overall F-test.

Emotion	Metric	Search engine	Mean	F-statistic[a]	P-value[a]
Meditation	Min	Bing	0.25	6.09	0.0038
		Google	0.27		
		Yahoo!	0.25		
	Max	Bing	0.44	4.68	0.0126
		Google	0.45		
		Yahoo!	0.49		
	Avg	Bing	0.33	2.19	0.1198
		Google	0.34		
		Yahoo!	0.34		
	Fluctuation	Bing	0.58	6.82	0.002
		Google	0.55		
		Yahoo!	0.70		

[a]F-test for null-hypothesis of no effect of *Search Engine*, from ANOVA with *Participant*, *Search Engine*, *Search Term* and *Occasion* as fixed effects; F-statistic has 2 and 66 degrees of freedom. Significant P-values ($P < 0.05$) are underlined.

For the emotion Meditation, the Minimum metric showed statistically significant differences ($P = 0.0038$), with Google having the greatest mean minimum (0.27), followed by Yahoo! and Bing having an average mean of 0.25. The Maximum metric also indicated statistically significant differences between the Search Engines ($P = 0.0126$). Bing had the lowest average mean (0.44), followed by Google (0.45) and Yahoo! (0.49). The Average metric did not show statistically significant differences. The Fluctuation metric showed statistically significant differences between search engines ($P = 0.002$). Google showed the lowest mean fluctuation (0.55), followed by Bing (0.58) and Yahoo! (0.70). The fact that Yahoo! had the greatest mean Fluctuation metric can probably be explained by the fact that this search engine had the greatest mean Maximum metric, and mean Average metrics did not differ significantly between search engines.

Effect of Search Term. The mean values and overall F-test for the effect of *Search Term* on BCI metrics for the emotion *Meditation* are displayed in Table 8.

For the emotion Meditation, the Minimum metric showed statistically significant differences between search terms ($P < 0.0001$), with Seal having the greatest mean minimum (0.27) followed by Shoot (0.26) and Divide (0.24). The Maximum metric did not indicate statistically significant differences between the Search Terms. The Average metric indicated statistically significant differences ($P = 0.0024$), with the Divide having the lowest average mean (0.33), followed by the Shoot (0.34) and Seal (0.35). The Fluctuation metric also showed statistically significant differences between search terms ($P < 0.0001$), with Shoot showing the lowest mean fluctuation (0.54) followed by

Table 8. Effect of search term on BCI metrics for the emotion *Meditation*: mean values and overall F-test.

Emotion	Metric	Search term	Mean	F-statistic[a]	P-value[a]
Meditation	Min	Shoot	0.26	13.79	<.0001
		Divide	0.24		
		Seal	0.27		
	Max	Shoot	0.44	2.71	0.0736
		Divide	0.48		
		Seal	0.46		
	Avg	Shoot	0.34	6.61	0.0024
		Divide	0.33		
		Seal	0.35		
	Fluctuation	Shoot	0.54	14.29	<.0001
		Divide	0.74		
		Seal	0.55		

[a]F-test for null-hypothesis of no effect of *Search Term*, from ANOVA with *Participant*, *Search Engine*, *Search Term* and *Occasion* as fixed effects; F-statistic has 2 and 66 degrees of freedom. Significant P-values ($P < 0.05$) are underlined.

Seal (0.55) and Divide (0.74). The fact that Divide had the greatest mean Fluctuation metric can probably be explained by the fact that this search term had the smallest mean Minimum metric.

Effect of Occasion. For the emotion Meditation, none of the metrics showed statistically significant differences between occasions.

7.5 Frustration

Effect of Search Engine. The mean values and overall F-test for the effect of *Search Engine* on BCI metrics for the emotion *Frustration* are displayed in Table 9.

For the emotion Frustration, the Minimum ($P = 0.0229$) and Fluctuation ($P = 0.0081$) metrics showed statistically significant differences between search engines. The Maximum and Average metrics did not show statistically significant differences. Google showed the greatest mean minimum (0.27), followed by Bing (0.25) and Yahoo! (0.20). Google showed the lowest mean fluctuation (1.28), followed by Bing (1.30) and Yahoo! (1.53). The fact that Yahoo! had the greatest mean Fluctuation metric can probably be explained by the fact that this search engine had the lowest mean Minimum metric, while the Maximum and Average metrics did not show statistically significant differences between search engines.

Table 9. Effect of search engine on BCI metrics for the Emotion *Frustration*: mean values and overall F-test.

Emotion	Metric	Search engine	Mean	F-statistic[a]	P-value[a]
Frustration	Min	Bing	0.25	4	0.0229
		Google	0.27		
		Yahoo!	0.20		
	Max	Bing	0.93	1.05	0.3572
		Google	0.93		
		Yahoo!	0.96		
	Avg	Bing	0.55	1.86	0.1636
		Google	0.56		
		Yahoo!	0.52		
	Fluctuation	Bing	1.30	5.18	0.0081
		Google	1.28		
		Yahoo!	1.53		

[a]F-test for null-hypothesis of no effect of *Search Engine*, from ANOVA with *Participant*, *Search Engine*, *Search Term* and *Occasion* as fixed effects; F-statistic has 2 and 66 degrees of freedom. Significant P-values ($P < 0.05$) are underlined.

Effect of Search Term. The mean values and overall F-test for the effect of *Search Term* on BCI metrics for the emotion *Frustration* are displayed in Table 10.

For the emotion Frustration, all of the metrics, Minimum ($P = 0.0017$), Maximum ($P = 0.0102$), Average ($P = 0.0072$) and Fluctuation ($P < 0.0001$), showed statistically significant differences between search terms. The Fluctuation metric for the search term Seal showed the lowest mean fluctuation (1.21), followed by Shoot (1.27) and Divide (1.62). This search term was also the only search term that required the participant to view four web pages before finding the correct answer.

Effect of Occasion. For the emotion Frustration, none of the metrics showed statistically significant differences between occasions.

Table 10. Effect of search term on BCI metrics for the emotion *Frustration*: mean values and overall F-test.

Emotion	Metric	Search term	Mean	F-statistic[a]	P-value[a]
Frustration	Min	Shoot	0.26	7.02	0.0017
		Divide	0.19		
		Seal	0.27		
	Max	Shoot	0.91	4.92	0.0102
		Divide	0.98		
		Seal	0.93		
	Avg	Shoot	0.54	5.32	0.0072
		Divide	0.51		
		Seal	0.58		
	Fluctuation	Shoot	1.27	12.86	<.0001
		Divide	1.62		
		Seal	1.21		

[a]F-test for null-hypothesis of no effect of *Search Term*, from ANOVA with *Participant, Search Engine, Search Term* and *Occasion* as fixed effects; F-statistic has 2 and 66 degrees of freedom. Significant P-values ($P < 0.05$) are underlined.

7.6 Discussion

The Minimum and Fluctuation metrics showed a statistically significant effect of Search Engine with regard to all emotions except Engagement. Similarly, the Minimum and Fluctuation metrics showed a statistically significant effect of Search Term with regard to all emotions. In contrast, the Average metric generally did not discriminate between search engines or search terms, with the exception of the emotions Meditation and Frustration where the Average metric showed significant differences between Search Terms.

Overall, therefore, of the four BCI metrics that were investigated (Minimum, Maximum, Average and Fluctuation), the Minimum seemed to be the most sensitive metric for discriminating between both Search Engines and Search Terms. When the Fluctuation metric showed significant differences, this was usually associated with significant differences in the Minimum metric, and differences (not always significant) in the Maximum metric. Thus high mean Fluctuation was usually associated with low mean Minimum values of the BCI measurement in question, and sometimes with high mean Maximum measurements.

With the exception of the Average metric for the emotion of Engagement, no significant effect of Occasion was seen for any BCI metric for any emotion. This finding suggests that learning or tiring effects generally did not affect the emotions, and BCI measurements taken on different occasions were generally comparable.

In summary, Search Engine had a statistically significant effect on the emotions Long-Term Excitement, Short-Term Excitement, Meditation and Frustration, whereas Search Term had a statistically significant effect on all of the emotions. In contrast, Occasion was only a significant factor for Engagement.

8 Conclusion

This study used a BCI to attempt to characterise the participants' UX of different search engines when they conducted WWW searches using ambiguous search queries.

The analysis of the pre-test questionnaire showed that less than half of the participants would give up searching for an answer after 10 min, and that more than half of them were not prepared to change their search queries more than twice. This could possibly be ascribed to participants getting frustrated with irrelevant results from the search engine, or from ambiguous search queries.

The statistical analysis of the BCI data showed that the specific search engine used was indeed a significant factor affecting the users' emotions. The exception to this finding was Engagement. The Search Term, however, significantly affected all emotions. As far as the factor Occasion is concerned, the order in which the search tasks were carried out did not significantly affect the users' emotions. This finding suggests that the participants' emotions were unaffected by learning or exhaustion effects.

The results from the post-test questionnaire indicated that 72% of the participants found the usability test exciting, with only 27% feeling frustrated. These findings contradicted the BCI data, which indicated that frustration was caused by the factors Search Engine and Search Term. This contradiction in results might be explained by the fact that the participants' responses were captured after completing the tasks. They could have felt more relaxed at that time, not remembering how they felt in the heat of the moment while performing the tasks, or not being willing to share their true emotions [34, 43]. Other explanations might be a bit more technical, involving the sensitivity of the Emotiv EPOC Neuroheadset's emotions measurements compared to the participants' emotional experiences, specifically in terms of Frustration, as explained by Nel, De Wet and Schall [25]. During the usability tests, the computer froze three times, and the recording software crashed four times. In each case, the test had to be restarted. These technical hitches caused by restart delays might have created some level of frustration. The post-test questionnaire results documented some participants (14%) were relieved when the test session was over − also an indication that frustration might have been present. However, the majority (61%) of the participants felt relaxed and were not bored (81%). They were generally positive towards the overall usability test, suggesting that their emotions did not negatively affect the reliability of the captured data.

To conclude, the findings of this study answered the research question in that Search Engine and Search Term did have significant effects on the BCI metrics for Long-Term Excitement, Short-Term Excitement, Engagement, Meditation and Frustration.

References

1. Albert, B.: Measuring emotional engagement. https://www.bentley.edu/files/2017/04/27/UXHongKong2017_Albert_Workshop.pdf. Accessed 15 Nov 2018

2. Alpert, J., Hajaj, N.: We knew the web was big. http://googleblog.blogspot.com/2008/07/we-knew-web-was-big.html. Accessed 26 Nov 2018
3. Azzopardi, L.: Position paper: towards evaluating the user experience of interactive information access systems. In: Proceedings of the SIGIR 2007 Workshop Web Information Seeking and Interaction, pp. 60–64 (2007)
4. Belkin, N.J.: Interaction with texts: information retrieval as information seeking behaviour. Inf. Retr. Boston **93**, 55–66 (1993)
5. Brandman, D.M., et al.: Rapid calibration of an intracortical brain–computer interface for people with tetraplegia. J. Neural Eng. **15**, 2 (2018)
6. Breytenbach, J., McDonald, T.: Soekenjindekking van Suid-Afrikaanse en Afrikaanse webruimtes. Suid-Afrikaanse Tydskr. vir Natuurwetenskap en Tegnol. **29**, 3 (2010)
7. Broder, A.: A taxonomy of web search. ACM SIGIR Forum **36**(2), 3–10 (2002). https://doi.org/10.1145/792550.792552
8. Carrol, J.M.: Beyond fun. Interactions **11**(5), 38–40 (2004)
9. Colman, J., Gnanayutham, P.: Assistive technologies for brain-injured gamers. In: Kouroupetroglou, G. (ed.) Assistive Technologies and Computer Access for Motor Disabilities, pp. 28–56. IGI Global, Hershey (2013)
10. Dou, Z., et al.: A large-scale evaluation and analysis of personalised search strategies. In: Proceedings of the 16th International Conference on World Wide Web - WWW 2007, p. 581 (2007). https://doi.org/10.1145/1242572.1242651
11. Edosomwan, O.J., Edosomwan, T.: Comparative analysis of some search engines. S. Afr. J. Sci. **106**(11/12), 1–4 (2010)
12. Elbassuoni, S., et al.: Adaptive personalisation of web search. In: Proceedings of the SIGIR 2007 Workshop Web Information Seeking and Interaction, pp. 1–4 (2007)
13. Emotiv: Emotiv EPOC and TestBench specifications (2014)
14. Emotiv: Emotiv EPOC specifications. Brain-computer interface technology. http://www.emotiv.com/upload/manual/sdk/EPOCSpecifications.pdf. Accessed 06 Feb 2014
15. Frakes, W.B., Baeza-Yates, R.: Information Retrieval: Data Structures and Algorithms. Prentice Hall (1992)
16. Gmac: Affectiv suite. http://emotiv.com/forum/messages/forum12/topic4084/message18512/?sphrase_id=1442#message18512. Accessed 15 Aug 2014
17. Goodman, E., Cramer, M.: The future of search. The emerging power of real-time personalised search (2010). http://www.comscore.com/Press_Events/Presentations_Whitepapers/2010/The_Future_of_Search_The_Emerging_Power_of_Real-time_Personalized_Search
18. Granka, L.A., et al.: Eye-tracking analysis of user behaviour in WWW search. In: Proceedings of the 27th Annual International ACM SIGIR Conference on Research and Development in Information Retrieval, Sheffield, South Yorkshire, UK, pp. 478–479 (2004). https://doi.org/10.1145/1008992.1009079
19. Hammer, E.M. et al.: Psychological predictors of visual and auditory P300 brain-computer interface performance. Front. Neurosci. **12**, 1–12 (2018). https://doi.org/10.3389/fnins.2018.00307
20. International Standards Organization - ISO FDIS 9241-210. (2009). Ergonomics of human system interaction - Part 210: Human-centered design for interactive systems. International Organization for Standardization (ISO), Switzerland
21. Kameswara Rao, T., et al.: An exploration on brain-computer interface and its recent trends. Int. J. Adv. Res. Artif. Intell. **1**(8), 17–22 (2012). https://doi.org/10.14569/ijarai.2012.010804
22. Kempthorne, O.: Design and Analysis of Experiments. Robert E Krieger Publishing Company, Florida (1983)
23. Luo, C., et al.: Query ambiguity identification based on user behaviour information. Inf. Retr. Technol. **863**, 36–47 (2014)

24. McCarthy, J., Wright, P.: Technology as Experience. MIT Press, Cambridge (2004)
25. Nel, W., et al.: The effect of search engine, search term and occasion on brain-computer interface metrics for emotions when ambiguous search queries are used. In: CHIRA 2019 - Proceedings of the 3rd International Conference on Computer-Human Interaction Research and Applications, Chira, pp. 28–39 (2019). https://doi.org/10.5220/0008164900280039
26. Nicolas-Alonso, L.F., Gomez-Gil, J.: Brain-computer interfaces, a review. Sensors 12(2), 1211–1279 (2012). https://doi.org/10.3390/s120201211
27. Nielsen, J., Norman, D.: The definition of user experience. http://www.nngroup.com/articles/definition-user-experience/. Accessed 12 Mar 2018
28. Oberoi, I.S., Chopra, M.: Web Search Engines – A Comparative Study (2010)
29. Preece, J., et al.: Interaction Design - Beyond Human-Computer Interaction. Wiley, West Sussex (2015)
30. Rawat, N.: What are some characteristics of web search engines? https://www.quora.com/What-are-some-characteristics-of-web-search-engines. Accessed 20 Aug 2018
31. Rogers, Y., et al.: Interaction Design - Beyond Human-Computer Interaction. Wiley, West Sussex (2011)
32. Rose, D.E., Levinson, D.: Understanding user goals in web search. In: The 13th International Conference on World Wide Web, New York, pp. 13–19 (2004). https://doi.org/10.1145/988672.988675
33. Sanderson, M.: Ambiguous queries: Test collections need more sense. In: Proceedings of the 31st Annual International ACM SIGIR Conference on Research and Development in Information Retrieval, pp. 499–506 (2008). https://doi.org/10.1145/1390334.1390420
34. Schall, A.: The future of UX research: uncovering the true emotions of our users (2015). http://uxpamagazine.org/the-future-of-ux-research/
35. Shah, J.J.: A Closed-Loop Brain-Computer Interface System: Hardware Implementation. San Diego State University (2018)
36. Song, R., et al.: Identification of ambiguous queries in web search. Inf. Process. Manag. 45(2), 216–229 (2009). https://doi.org/10.1016/j.ipm.2008.09.005
37. Song, R., et al.: Identifying ambiguous queries in web search. In: Proceedings of the 16th International Conference on World Wide Web - WWW 2007, p. 1169 (2007). https://doi.org/10.1145/1242572.1242749
38. Steyrl, D., et al.: On similarities and differences of invasive and non-invasive electrical brain signals in brain-computer interfacing. J. Biomed. Sci. Eng. 9(9), 393–398 (2016). https://doi.org/10.4236/jbise.2016.98034
39. Takahashi, K., et al.: The response of eye-movement and pupil size to audio instruction while viewing a moving target. In: Proceedings of the Eye-Tracking Research and Applications Symposium, Palm Beach Gardens, FL, USA (2000)
40. Teevan, J., et al.: Characterising the value of personalising search. In: SIGIR 2007 (2007)
41. Thorpe, J., et al.: Pass-thoughts: authenticating with our minds. Presented at the (2005). https://doi.org/10.1145/1146269.1146282
42. Trimmer, P.C., et al.: On the evolution and optimality of mood states. Behav. Sci. (Basel) 3(3), 501–521 (2013). https://doi.org/10.3390/bs3030501
43. Tullis, T., Albert, B.: Measuring the User Experience - Collecting, Analyzing, and Presenting Usability Metrics. Elsevier/Morgan Kaufmann, Amsterdam (2013)
44. User Experience Professionals Association: Definitions of user experience and usability. https://uxpa.org/resources/definitions-user-experience-and-usability. Accessed 12 Mar 2018
45. Waldert, S.: Invasive vs non-invasive neuronal signals for brain-machine interfaces: will one prevail? Front. Neurosci. 10, 1–4 (2016). https://doi.org/10.3389/fnins.2016.00295
46. Wolpaw, J.R., et al.: Brain-computer interfaces for communication and control. Clin. Neurophysiol. 113(6), 767–791 (2002). https://doi.org/10.1016/S1388-2457(02)00057-3

47. Ying, K., et al.: Emotional UX – Techniques for measuring user's emotions. https://eyetracking.com.sg/2015/12/15/emotional-ux-techniques-for-measuring-users-emotions/. Accessed 16 Nov 2018

48. Liu, Y., Scheuermann, P., Li, X., Zhu, X.: Using WordNet to disambiguate word senses for text classification. In: Shi, Y., van Albada, G.D., Dongarra, J., Sloot, P.M.A. (eds.) ICCS 2007. LNCS, vol. 4489, pp. 781–789. Springer, Heidelberg (2007). https://doi.org/10.1007/978-3-540-72588-6_127

49. Bing search engine. www.bing.com. Accessed 26 Nov 2018

50. Frequency bands - What are they and how do I access them? https://emotiv.zendesk.com/hc/en-us/articles/208378593-Frequency-Bands-what-are-they-and-how-do-I-access-them. Accessed 11 Nov 2018

51. Google Search Engine. www.google.co.za. Accessed 26 Nov 2018

52. Short history of early search engines. http://www.thehistoryofseo.com/The-Industry/Short_History_of_Early_Search_Engines.aspx. Accessed 12 Sept 2017

53. The history of search engines - An infographic. http://www.wordstream.com/articles/internet-search-engines-history. Accessed 12 Sept 2017

54. Yahoo! Search Engine. https://za.yahoo.com/. Accessed 26 Nov 2018

Taxonomized Auditory Distractions with Varying Intensity Levels and Their Effect on a Visual P300 Speller While Utilising Low-Cost off-the-Shelf Equipment

Patrick Schembri$^{(\boxtimes)}$ ⓘ, Mariusz Pelc ⓘ, and Jixin Ma ⓘ

Department of Computer and Information Systems, University of Greenwich, Greenwich London, UK
{P.Schembri,M.Pelc,J.Ma}@greenwich.ac.uk

Abstract. This paper introduces a hierarchical taxonomy for different categories of distractions that are commonly encountered in a real-life environment. In this work, we implicitly focus on auditory distractions with contrasting intensity levels, explicitly that of no music (*M0*), music at 30% (*M30*), music at 60% (*M60*), and music at 90% (*M90*) i.e. our independent variables, and the effect that these distractions have on our dependent variables i.e. amplitude, latency, accuracy, user preference and signal morphology while using a visual P300 Speller. The research method for this study includes the use of a visual P300 speller based on the oddball paradigm in conjunction with the xDAWN algorithm. This work employed the use of N = 10 healthy subjects while utilizing low-cost electroencephalographic (EEG) equipment. This study forms part of a series of studies based on EEG, focused on ensuing in the development of the aforementioned taxonomy. Our results show that for the accuracy dependent variable, the *M0* at 100% was preeminent, trailed surprisingly by *M90* at 98%, and equally by *M60* and *M30* at 96%. The subjects' preference prodigiously shows that the preferred condition was *M0* as originally expected, followed by *M90*, *M60*, and *M30*, which are inadvertently in the same order to the accuracy dependent variable. Statistical analysis between all independent variables accepts our null hypothesis for the amplitude and latency. Other statistical results such as the comparison of each independent variable with *M0* is included in this paper. The results from this work should give an overview of the viability and feasibility of the aforementioned P300 speller methodology and equipment to be utilized in the real-world environment.

Keywords: Brain-Computer Interface (BCI) · Electroencephalography (EEG) · Event-Related Potential (ERP) · P300 speller (P3) · Distractions · Taxonomy

1 Introduction

In the context of Brain-Computer Interfaces (BCI), distractions are unwanted since these may shift the subjects' attention from the task at hand i.e. from the experiment that is being performed. As such, current practices in BCI is to mitigate or eliminate distractions

© Springer Nature Switzerland AG 2021
M. J. Escalona et al. (Eds.): CHIRA 2018/CHIRA 2019, CCIS 1351, pp. 124–141, 2021.
https://doi.org/10.1007/978-3-030-67108-2_7

by careful designing and meticulous planning of the experiments. The work presented herein is part of a larger based BCI project and in continuation of our previous and latest papers [1, 2], with the goal of building a hierarchal taxonomy, as portrayed in Fig. 1, aimed at categorizing different types of distractions that are commonly encountered in a real-life environment, and their effects thereof. In addition, this paper is an extension of work originally presented in [3], which is also in continuation of the aforementioned papers, and in preceding one of our latest paper [4].

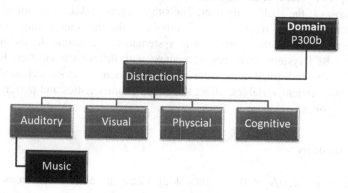

Fig. 1. Establishing and development of an extensible P300b hierarchal taxonomy to categorize different types of distractions encountered in a real-world context [3].

The research and development of BCI have been principally focused on the speed of detection and accuracy of the application rather than its practicability for real-world environments. As a matter of fact, the majority of BCI experiments were and are still being performed in lab conditions, where the subject sits in a sound-attenuated room without any distractions such as [5, 6], which in the context of real-world practice is unrealistic. There are a handful of research papers that focus on real-world contexts such as [7, 8], however, their focus was either on auditory ERPs such as [9] or using medical-grade equipment such as [10].

Our goal is to analyze the effect that distractions have on the signal characteristics of a P300 component while using the P300 Speller paradigm alongside the development of a hierarchal taxonomy. In this paper, we introduce the concept and implicitly focus on a specific auditory distraction with varying level of intensities, explicitly that of No Music – Lab Condition (*M0*), Music at 30% (*M30*), Music at 60% (*M60*), and Music at 90% (*M90*) i.e. our independent variables. We then analyze the effect that each intensified distraction have on a visual P300 speller in terms of accuracy, amplitude, latency, user preference, signal morphology, and overall signal quality i.e. our dependent variables. The results are achieved by performing several statistical and non-statistical analysis, and through empirical evidence. In addition, our research makes use of non-invasive Brain-Computer Interface (BCI) on the basis of Electroencephalography (EEG).

The requirement for this work was derived from the need to broaden the utilization of this technology for both subjects with neuromuscular disabilities and healthy individuals, by providing a solution which is assessed outside lab conditions i.e. into noisy environments, and based on low-cost equipment. In the absence of comprehensive studies on the effect that distractions have in relation to the P300 performance i.e. for accuracy and signal characteristics, an evident necessity for this study was present. Our null hypothesis based on previous research [3] is that this type of distraction does not show any statistically significant effect on accuracy, task performance, amplitude, latency or signal morphology.

In this paper, we report a study where ten healthy subjects used Farwell and Donchin [11] P300 speller paradigm in conjunction with the xDAWN algorithm [12] while utilizing low-cost off-the-shelf equipment. The subjects were asked to communicate five alphanumeric characters, referred to as symbols, in the different settings mentioned above. The main aim of this study was to systematically examine the usability of a P300 Speller BCI system, in a specific context with different intensities. Empirical experiments were performed to measure how environmental factors such as the aforementioned independent variables, affect the signal characteristics and performance of the P300 component.

2 Methodology

The following segment/s of the methodology is/are the author's previous work as referenced above and are adopted and outlined in the current paper for readers' convenience.

2.1 Hardware

Our work utilizes the OpenBCI 32-bit board (dubbed Cyton) in conjunction with the Electro-Cap, which in the context of EEG experiments, is based on the international 10/20 system for electrode placement on the scalp.

The PIC32MX250F128B microcontroller found on the Cyton board has a 32-bit processor with a 50 MHz ceiling, and 32 KB of memory storage, while being Arduino compatible. It also encompasses an ADS1299 IC which is an 8-Channel, 24-Bit, simultaneous sampling delta-sigma, Analogue-to-Digital Converter used for biopotential measurements, developed by Texas Instruments. In addition, it has an in-built low-cost microcontroller, the RFDuino RFD22301, for wireless communication which communicates with the provided and pre-programmed USB dongle. In our previous paper [15], the reader can obtain a more in-depth elucidation of the Cyton board and it's built-in hardware components.

In addition, our work utilizes the Electro-Cap, which is made of fabric, explicitly that of elastic spandex. The electrodes which are directly attached to the afore fabric are made of pure tin and considered as wet electrodes. This implies that an electrolyte gel must be applied to the electrodes to have effective scalp contact. Otherwise, we could end up with impedance instability.

To output our three diverse distractions i.e. music at 30%, music at 60%, and music at 90%, we have used a pair of Creative Labs SBS 15 speakers, which can output a nominal (RMS) power of 5 W for each speaker, which have a frequency response of 90 Hz–20000 Hz, and a 90 dB SNR.

2.2 Participants

For this session, we enrolled N = 10 healthy subjects of which seven were males and three were females. They were aged between 29 and 38, with a mean of M = 33.8, and their participation was on a voluntary basis. Nine of the ten subjects native language was Maltese, while the native language for the latter subject was English.

However, all subjects in both sessions were au fait in the English language and were conversant with the alphanumeric symbols portrayed on the P300 Speller application. In addition, all subjects had previous experience using P300-BCI experiments.

Another subject aided in the groundwork and initial testing for the configuration of our equipment, and in the development of the methodology, however, he/she did not partake in the official experiments and hence his/her data is not included in the results.

2.3 Data Acquisition

We have set the sampling rate and sampling precision for the EEG signal at the hardware's ceiling of 250 Hz and 24-bit respectively. The raw data was stored anonymously in OpenVIBE .ov format, however, for offline analysis, this was converted to a comma-separated value (CSV) and imported in MATLAB. The stored raw data included the readings of eight EEG electrodes, namely, C3, Cz, C4, P3, Pz, P4, O1 and O2 which were placed in accordance to the International 10–20 System.

Since the spatial amplitude dispersal of the P300 component is symmetric around Cz and its electrical potential is maximal in the midline region (Cz, Pz) [16], we have opted to use the aforementioned electrodes. In addition and in view of the fact that, in general, an earlobe or a mastoid reference generates a robust P300 response, we have opted for a referential montage, with the reference electrode being placed on the left earlobe (A1), and the ground electrode being placed on the right ear lobe (A2).

2.4 P300 Speller and XDAWN

In this work, we utilize Farewell & Donchin P300 speller in combination with the xDAWN algorithm. This type of methodology is based on visual stimuli which are explained thoroughly below. The subject was presented with thirty-six symbols i.e. alphanumeric characters, which were positioned in a six by six grid dubbed as the spelling grid. The subject is asked to observe the intensification of each row and column, which for one repetition entails the intensification of six rows and six columns in random order. Then, the subject is asked to differentiate between a rare stimulus (target) which generates a spontaneous and exogenous ERP known as the P300 potential and a common stimulus (nontarget) which does not generate this component. This is achieved with the subject focusing his attention on the desired symbol (target) while ignoring the other symbols (nontarget). This implies that there will be one target column and one target row, while there will be five nontarget columns and five nontarget rows, for each repetition. The intersection of the row and column targets will predict what symbol was spelt for that repetition. In simplest terms, the prediction will distinguish between target i.e. a row or column stimuli that produce a P300 component from the non-target i.e. a row or column stimuli that do not produce a P300 component. Taking into consideration that the peak potential of P300 component is between 5-10 μV and that this is entrenched and concealed by artefacts and other brain activities, where the typical EEG signal is $\pm$100 μV; this implies that it would be very hard to predict the correct symbol with one repetition. This also leads to a very low Signal-to-Noise ratio and the most popular and established way to address this issue, is that for each symbol to be spelt numerous consecutive times i.e. more than one repetition per symbol, and then, average the corresponding column and/or row epochs over a number of repetitions, thus cancelling components unrelated to stimulus onset.

The xDAWN is a process of spatial filtering where (1) it is a dimensional reduction method that produces a subset of pseudo-channels, dubbed output channels, by a linear combination of the original channels and (2) it promotes the appealing part of the signal, such as ERPs, with respect to the noise. The process of xDAWN is applied to the date prior to any classification, for instance, LDA (Linear Discriminant Analysis) which was used for this work. From an abstract point of view, the xDAWN algorithm can be divided into (1) a least-square estimation of the evoked responses and (2) a generalized Rayleigh quotient to estimate a set of spatial filters that maximize the SSNR.

The following is adapted from [10] and [17]. Let $\mathbf{X} \in \mathbb{R}^{S \times C}$ be the EEG data that contain ERPs and noise, with S samples and C channels. Let $\mathbf{A} \in \mathbb{R}^{E \times C}$ be the matrix of ERP signals, while E is the number of temporal samples of the ERP (typically, E is chosen to correspond to 600 ms or 1 s). Let $\mathbf{N} \in \mathbb{R}^{S \times C}$ be the noise matrix which contains normally distributed noise. The ERPs position in the data is given by a Toeplitx matrix $\mathbf{D} \in \mathbb{R}^{E \times S}$. The data model is given by $\mathbf{X} = \mathbf{D^T A} + \mathbf{N}$. $\mathbf{A}$ is estimated by a least square estimate using a matrix inverse (pseudoinverse) as shown in formula (1).

$$\widehat{A} = \arg\min_{A} = ||X - DA||_2^2 = \left(D^T D\right)^{-1} D^T X \tag{1}$$

Let $\mathbf{W} \in \mathbb{R}^{S \times F}$ be the pseudo-channels while F represents the filters for projection. The result is the filtered data matrix $\tilde{\mathbf{X}} = \mathbf{XW}$. According to [10], the optimal filters W can be found by maximizing the SSNR as given by the generalized Rayleigh quotient:

$$\widehat{W} = \arg\max_{W} = \frac{Tr\left(W^T \widehat{A}^T D^T D \widehat{A} W\right)}{Tr\left(W^T X^T X W\right)} \tag{2}$$

The optimization problem is solved by combining a QRD (QR matrix decomposition) with an SVD (singular value decomposition). A more thorough explanation is found at [12].

2.5 Experimental Design

In this work, we had four independent variables manipulated: (a) Music at 0% (*M0*) (b) Music at 30% (*M30*), (c) Music at 60% (*M60*), and (d) Music at 90% (*M90*), within-subjects variables. Moreover, we had several dependent measures which were classified into three types of dependent variables i.e. online performance which comprised of the accuracy, offline performance which consisted of amplitude and latency, and user preference.

Independent Variables. As previously mentioned, we made use of four manipulated independent within-subjects variables, which are itemized and elucidated below. It is important to remember that all auditory distractions were performed from the same recording, with the same equipment and at the same level of intensity unless noted otherwise.

1. Music at 0% abridged as *M0* (or known as Lab Condition), where the experiments were performed in a sound-attenuated room, without any distractions.
2. Music at 30% volume abridged as *M30*, where the volume level was labelled as 'low' i.e. between 20 and 30 dB and simulated background music.
3. Music at 60% volume abridged as *M60*, where the volume level was labelled as 'medium' i.e. between 50 and 60 dB and simulated active listening to a movie.
4. Music at 90% volume abridged as *M90*, where the volume level was labelled as 'high' i.e. between 80 and 90 dB and simulated disco level music only i.e. there was no crowd chatter or other type of noise.

The comparison between Independent Variables was done as follows: *M0* versus *M30*, *M0* versus *M60*, *M0* versus *M90* respectively, and as combined results i.e. *M0* versus *M30* versus *M60* versus *M90*, *and M30* versus *M60* versus *M90*, for the dependent variables of amplitude and latency. The setting and configuration for all independent variables were outputted from a recorded simulation by the aforementioned speakers, with the volume set at the different levels as elucidated above. We have opted to use a recording and the same recording for all subjects since we are aiming in making the experiments between subjects as similar as possible. Moreover, this will make it possible to increase the level of volume equally in every experiment.

Dependent Variables. In this work, there were three types of dependent measures, which can be sub-categorized into four distinct dependent variables:

1. Online performance comprised of accuracy, which is the correctly spelt symbols when compared to the planned target symbols i.e. in our experiments we had 5 planned target symbols – BRAIN.
2. Offline statistics comprised of amplitude and latency, which (a) P300 amplitude (μV) is related to the distribution of the subject's processing resources assigned to the task. It is defined as the voltage difference between the largest positive peak from the baseline within the P300 latency interval. (b) P300 latency is considered a measure of cognitive processing time, generally between 300–800 ms [18] poststimulus i.e. after target stimulus. In simplest terms, it is the time interval between the onset of the target stimulus and the peak of the wave.
3. User preference, where two questionnaires were provided to the subjects to ask for their favourite usage condition. This was ranked from four to one, four being the highest and one being the lowest.

2.6 Experimental Design

An induction session was held for each subject which was intended to re-educate the subjects on the P300 speller paradigm and hardware being used. We also notified the subjects' that:

1. they would be doing the P300 speller experiment in five unique settings for the first session i.e. (i) the training phase which was performed in lab conditions i.e. in a sound-attenuated room (ii) *M0*, (iii) *M30*, (iv) *M60* and (v) *M90*, as elucidated in the independent variables.
2. they would be spelling the symbols "BRAIN" for (1 ii) to (1 v), while for (1 i) i.e. the training phase, they would be spelling fifteen random symbols.

The first experiment was always the training phase i.e. (1 i) since this was required as a training for the system to be able to predict correct symbols in the following experiments. Then, (1 ii) to (1 v), were done in a randomized order to circumvent the subjects accustomization to that particular distraction. Then, the subjects were asked if they had any queries which were promptly answered at this stage. The subject was then asked to be seated and relax for a few minutes prior to the start of the experiments. The setup was as follows: (a) the subject was seated facing the display, approximately one meter away, (b) the researcher was situated at the left-hand side of the subject and refrained for making any type of movement or noise throughout. We have opted to stay on the side of the subject, since from our experience and subjects feedback, they were not comfortable with someone being behind them, (c) the speakers were placed at a 15-degree angle facing the subject and where situated near the monitor i.e. one meter away from the subject, and (d) the electrode impedance was verified to be less than 5 KΩ. The experiment was only started when the subject had no additional questions, was in a comfortable position and was able to perform the task at hand.

Subsequently, the spelling grid consisting of 36 symbols in a 6 × 6 matrix was presented to the subjects and the target symbol i.e. the symbol the subject must focus on, was preceded by a cue i.e. the target symbol was highlighted in blue. Next, there was a random intensification of 100 ms for each row and column in the matrix and there was an 80 ms delay between two successive intensifications i.e. after one column and one row was intensified. This implies that we had an interstimulus interval (ISI) of 180 ms. Afterwards and to predict each symbol, there were fifteen repetitions (i.e. one trial) which consisted of intensifying six rows and six columns for each repetition, and in between each of the group of six rows and six columns i.e. one repetition, there was an inter-repetition delay of 100 ms. At the end of trial i.e. 6 rows × 6 columns × 15 repetitions, the symbol which was predicted by the system was presented to the subject by being highlighted with a green cue. The subject would be aware if the system predicted the correct target symbol. Moreover, in between trials i.e. in between different symbols, there was a 3000 ms inter-trial period. After the end of each experiment, the subjects were given a short break.

As previously mentioned, the training phase (1 i) was made up of one session that consisted of 15 random symbols by 15 trials each (i.e. 6 rows and 6 columns per trial * 15 trials = 180 flashes per symbol), and this took approximately 10 min. The *M0*, *M30*,

M60, and *M90* were made up of one session each and consisted of 5 specific symbols that make up the word "BRAIN", and similarly to the training phase, each symbol had 15 trials, with 6 rows and 6 columns per trial i.e. 180 flashes per symbol, and took approximately 6 min for each independent variable.

In total, we had 15 symbols which were spelt in the training phase, and 5 symbols which were spelt in the other aforementioned independent variables. Hence due to the matrix disposition, for the training phase, we had 2700 flashes of which 450 were targets and 2250 were nontargets, and 900 flashes per independent variable of which 150 were targets and 750 were nontargets. These values are per subject, while the data was store anonymously and the subjects were referred to as subject *x*.

2.7 Signal Processing – Online

The OpenViBE 2.0.0 was selected as our online system which also takes care of the raw signal acquisition. This application is designed for processing of real-time biosignal data, is a C++ based software platform, and is well known for its graphical language to design signal processing chains. It has two main components called the acquisition server, which interfaces with the Cyton board, reads the raw data signal and produces a uniform signal stream which is transmitted to the designer, which in turn is composed of several scenarios where we can structure, construct and execute signal processing chains.

The acquisition server takes care of obtaining the signal from the Cyton board, however, it does not communicate with the board directly, instead, it provides dedicated drivers to perform this task. The sampling rate of the signal was set at 250 Hz, and consisted of 8 EEG channels and 3 auxiliary channels, with the latter channels being used to broadcast data from the accelerometer. In a single buffer and with accepted values being only powers-of-two, explicitly from 2^2 to 2^9, we set the *sample count per sent block* to 32, which implies how many samples need to be sent per channel. In addition, the cyton board reply reading timeout was regulated at 5000 ms, while the flushing timeout was adjusted to 500 ms. Although the version of OpenVibe that we are using depends on TCP tagging to align the EEG signal with the simulation markers, we had set the drift tolerance to 20 ms. The issue with this setting is that it can introduce signal artefacts and mask other possible faults such as driver issues. Even though these issues were not encountered in this work, we have decided to discontinue the use of drift tolerance in future experiments, since when TCP tagging was introduced, it made the drift tolerance mechanism redundant. The P300 speller paradigm was managed by the *designer* in which there were a number of scenarios that were executed in order as thoroughly explained below:

The *first scenario* was the acquisition of the signal and stimuli markers for the training phase. The recordings included the raw EEG and stimuli.

The *second scenario* entailed the pre-processing of the signal where it trained the spatial filter using the xDAWN algorithm. The subjects' data recorded in the training session was utilized, with the following configuration and modalities. Initially, we have chosen to eliminate the last three auxiliary channels which stored the auxiliary data of the accelerometer since the board was firmly placed on the desk and this information was not required. Subsequently, a Butterworth bandpass filter of 1 Hz–20 Hz was applied with an order of 5 and a ripple (dB) of 0.5 to remove the DC offset, the 50 Hz (60 Hz in some countries) electrical interference, any signal harmonics and unnecessary frequencies which are not beneficial in our experiments. Next, no signal decimation was used since the sampling rate and count per buffer previously used in the acquisition server were not compatible with the actual signal decimation factor due to the Cyton board's sampling rate of 250 Hz (no available value in the sample count per block is factorable with 250 Hz). However, we still passed the signal through *time-based epoching* which generated 'epochs' (signal slices) with a duration of 0.25 s and time offset of 0.25 s between epochs (i.e. we created a temporal buffer to collect the data and forward them into blocks). This implies that there was no overlapping of data and that the inputs for the *xDAWN spatial filter* and the *Stimulation based epoching* were based on epochs of 0.25 s rather than the whole data. In simplest terms, we had one point for every 0.25 s of data which made our signal coarser. Subsequently, we passed the time-based epochs and stimulations to the *Stimulation based epoching* which sliced the signal into chunks of the desired length following a stimulation event. This had an epoch duration of 0.6 s (p300 deviation around 0.3 s after the stimuli) and no offset. Lastly, the stimulations, time-based epochs and the stimulation based epochs were passed to the xDAWN trainer which in simplest terms trains spatial filters that best highlight ERPs. The xDAWN expression, utilized in OpenVIBE, which has to be maximized, varies marginally from the original xDAWN (Rivet et al., 2009) formula where the numerator includes only the average of the target signals. In addition, the implemented algorithm maximizes the quantity via a generalized eigenvalue decomposition method in which the best spatial filters are given by the eigenvectors corresponding to the largest eigenvalues (Clerc et al., 2016). This scenario created twenty-four coefficients values in sequence (i.e. 8 input channels by 3 output channels) that were used in the following scenario.

The *third scenario* carried on the pre-processing of the signal where it trained the classifier, partially with the values from the previous scenario. Once again the subjects' raw data which was recorded in the training session was utilized with the elimination of the last three aux channels, the omission of signal decimation and the application of a Butterworth bandpass filter of 1 Hz-20 Hz; identical to the previous scenario. Subsequently the parameters of the xDAWN spatial filter that were generated in the second scenario which include the 24 spatial filter coefficients, 8 input channels and output 3 output channels. This spatial filter generated 3 output channels from the original 8 input channels, where each output channel was a linear combination of the input channels. The output channels were computed by performing the "sum on i ($Cij * Ii$)" as shown in formula (3), where Ii represents the input channel (n is set to 8), Oj represents the output channel and Cij is the coefficient of the ith input channel and jth output channel in the spatial filter matrix.

$$Oj = \sum_{i=1}^{n} Cij * Ii \tag{3}$$

Subsequently, the outputted signals (i.e. the 3 output channels) and the stimulations were passed equivalently into two separate *stimulation based epoching*; for the target and the non-target selection. These had an epoch duration of 0.6 s and no offset. The output i.e. both epoch signals (target and non-target) were again separately computed with block averaging and passed through a feature aggregator that combined the received input features into a feature vector that was used for the classification. This implies that two separate feature vector streams were outputted; the target and non-target selections. Ultimately both vector streams and the stimulations were passed through our *classifier trainer*. We have opted to pass all the data through a single classifier trainer, hence the native multiclass strategy was chosen, which used the classifier training algorithm without a pairwise strategy. The algorithm chosen for our classifier is the regular LDA. The output at this stage is a trained classifier with the settings outputted to a file for use in the next scenario.

The *fourth scenario* consisted of the actual online experiments and was more complex since it was necessary to collect data, pre-process it, classify it and provide online feedback to the subject. The front-end consisted of displaying the 6 × 6 grid, flashing rows and columns and give feedback to the subject. The back-end consisted of a number of processes. Primarily, the data was acquired from the subject in real-time and similar to what was done in the previous scenarios, the last three aux channels were eliminated, signal decimation was omitted, a Butterworth bandpass filter of 1 Hz–20 Hz was used and the parameters of the xDAWN spatial filter that were generated in the *second scenario* which included the twenty-four spatial filter coefficients were used. Subsequently, the output and the stimulations were passed in the *Stimulation based epoching* which had epoch duration of 0.6 s and no offset. This was then averaged and passed through a *feature aggregator* to produce a feature vector for the classifier. Lastly, the *classifier processor* classifies the incoming feature vectors by using the previously learned classifier (*classifier trainer*).

The *fifth scenario* allows us to replay the experiments by selecting the raw data file and re-processing the functions of the fourth scenario.

2.8 Signal Processing – Online

In the offline analysis, the following procedure was done for each *M0, M30, M60*, and *M90*. The captured raw data was converted from the proprietary OpenVIBE *.ov* extension to a more commonly used *.csv* format using a particular scenario aimed for this task. The outputs were two files in *.csv* format which contained the raw data and stimulations respectively. These were later imported into MATLAB R2014a tables called *samples* and *stims* and then converted to arrays. Subsequently, any unnecessary rows and columns in the *samples* array were removed. These consisted of the first rows which contained the time header, channel names and sampling rate; the first column which contained the time(s) and the last three columns which stored the auxiliary data of the accelerometer. Next, we filtered out the *stims* array to include the target stimulations with code (33285); non-target stimulations (33286); visual stimulation stop (32780), which is the start of each flash of row or column; and segment start (32771), which is the start of each trial (12 flashes, 6 rows and 6 columns make up 1 trial). Additional data such as the *sampleTime*, *samplingFreq* and *channelNames* variables were extracted from the data and stored in the workspace. Subsequently, we had to perform a signal inversion due to the hardware and driver implementation.

The *samples* array was later imported into EEGLAB for processing and for offline analysis. The first process was to apply a bandpass filter of 1–20 Hz to eliminate the environmental electrical interference (50 Hz or 60 Hz dependent on the country), to remove any signal harmonics and unnecessary frequencies which are not beneficial in our experiments and to remove the DC offset. Subsequently, we import the event info (the stimulations – *stim* array) in EEGLAB with the format {*latency, type, duration*} in milliseconds.

Next, the imported data was used in ERPLAB which is an add-on of EEGLAB and is targeted for ERP analysis. Although the dataset in EEGLAB already contains information about all the individual events, we have created an *eventlist* structure in ERPLAB that consolidates this information and makes it easier to access and display; and also allows ERPLAB to add additional information which is not present in the original EEGLAB list of events. Subsequently, we take every event we want to average together and assign that to a specific bin via the *binlister*. This contained an abstract description of what kinds of event codes go into a particular bin. In our experiments we have used the following criteria: ".{33285}{t <50-150> 32780}"for the target and ".{33286}{t <50-150> 32780}" for the non-target. This implies that it is time-locked to the stimuli event 33285 (target) or 33286 (non-target) and must have the event 32780 that happens 50 to 150 ms after the target/non-target event. If this criterion is met, it is placed in the appropriate BIN.

Subsequently, we extracted the bin-based epochs via ERPLAB (not the EEGLAB version) and set the time period from -0.2 s before the stimulus until 0.8 s after the stimulus. We have also used baseline correction (pre) since we wanted to subtract the average pre-stimulus voltage from each epoch of data. Next, we passed all channels epoch data through a moving window peak-to-peak threshold artefact detection with the voltage threshold set at 100 μV, moving window width at 200 ms and window step at 100 ms to remove unwanted signals such as blinking and moving artefacts. Lastly, we averaged our dataset ERPs and performed an average across ERPsets (Grand Average) to produce the results shown in Table 6 and 7, generated by the ERP measurement tool.

3   Results

In this section, we present several results in relation to the dependent variables such as a one-way ANOVA to determine the effect that *M0, M30, M60,* and *M90* distractions have on the online performance (accuracy), offline statistics (amplitude and latency) and user preference. In the following tables the labels *M0, M30, M60,* and *M90* represent "music at 0% i.e. lab condition", "music at 30%", "music at 60%", and "music at 90%" distractions as thoroughly explained beforehand.

3.1   Online Analysis

Following the online experiments, the results achieved per subject are shown in Table 1 which depicts the predicted symbols out of five, and the percentage in parentheses, rounded to the nearest one, for the accuracy dependent variable. It must be noted that in an incorrect symbol prediction, it might be the case that the column was predicted correctly, whilst the row was predicted incorrectly or vice versa. For instance, subject9 had a success rate of 80% in the *M30* scenario, with the symbol R predicted as symbol F i.e. the column prediction was correct but not the row. However, to avoid ambiguity we have decided to assume that both row and column prediction were incorrect when the symbol is predicted incorrectly.

Table 1. Symbols spelt (out of 5) and percentage (in parentheses) for the accuracy dependent variable.

S	M0	M30	M60	M90
S1	5 (100%)	5 (100%)	4 (80%)	5 (100%)
S2	5 (100%)	5 (100%)	4 (80%)	4 (80%)
S3	5 (100%)	5 (100%)	5 (100%)	5 (100%)
S4	5 (100%)	5 (100%)	5 (100%)	5 (100%)
S5	5 (100%)	5 (100%)	5 (100%)	5 (100%)
S6	5 (100%)	5 (100%)	5 (100%)	5 (100%)
S7	5 (100%)	5 (100%)	5 (100%)	5 (100%)
S8	5 (100%)	4 (80%)	5 (100%)	5 (100%)
S9	5 (100%)	4 (80%)	5 (100%)	5 (100%)
S10	5 (100%)	5 (100%)	5 (100%)	5 (100%)
Average	100%	96%	96%	98%

3.2 Offline Analysis

In this section, we process and analyze the averaged epoch signal of ten subjects in relation to the independent variables ($M0$, $M30$, $M60$, and $M90$). We have performed three separate one-way ANOVAs on the amplitude and latency dependent variables where (a) Table 2 depicts $M0$ versus $M30$, (b) Table 3 depicts $M0$ versus $M60$, and (c) Table 4 depicts $M0$ versus $M90$. We have chosen to use a 5% significance level (0.05) denoted as α (alpha) and rounded all values to the nearest thousandth.

Table 2. One-way ANOVA statistical analysis on Amplitude and Latency – $M0$ versus $M30$.

	Source of Variation	SS	df	MS	F	P-value	F Crit
Amplitude	BG	0.158	1	0.158	0.127	0.726	4.414
	WG	22.486	18	1.249			
	Total	22.644	19				
Latency	BG	987.013	1	987.013	1.681	0.211	4.414
	WG	10571.625	18	587.313			
	Total	11558.638	19				

Table 3. One-way ANOVA statistical analysis on Amplitude and Latency – *M0* versus *M60*.

	Source of Variation	SS	df	MS	F	P-value	F Crit
Amplitude	BG	0.528	1	0.528	0.554	0.466	4.414
	WG	17.164	18	0.954			
	Total	17.692	19				
Latency	BG	1224.613	1	1224.613	2.013	0.173	4.414
	WG	10947.825	18	608.213			
	Total	12172.438	19				

Table 4. One-way ANOVA statistical analysis on Amplitude and Latency – *M0* versus *M90*.

	Source of Variation	SS	df	MS	F	P-value	F Crit
Amplitude	BG	0.001	1	0.001	0.002	0.969	4.414
	WG	16.878	18	0.938			
	Total	16.879	19				
Latency	BG	793.8	1	793.8	1.174	0.293	4.414
	WG	12165.75	18	675.875			
	Total	12959.55	19				

Our null hypothesis (H_0) states that the means are all equal per table i.e. the mean between *M0* and *M30*, *M0* and *M60*, and *M0* and *M90*, is the same. Our alternate hypothesis (H_1) states that at least two of these means are different. Even though we are comparing only two groups, we have opted to use one-way ANOVA rather than a T-test for comparison between results [3] and to avoid a statistical Type I error on multiple two-sample T-tests. Regardless, this should yield the same results.

For instance, consider the results for Table 2 in the amplitude section. The acronyms *BG* stands for Between Groups while *WG* stands for Within Groups. In the first column we have the source of variation, where ANOVA carries out an analysis between groups variation i.e. *M0* and *M30*, and also carry out an analysis of the within-groups variation i.e. the variation within each of our two groups. In the second column, we have the sum of squares (*SS*) of the variation, which is the spread between each individual value and the mean. The third column is the degrees of freedom (*df*) which is the (number of samples – 1). We have two samples of between groups which gives one and we have twenty samples in total which give nineteen. That allows us to calculate the within-group *df* which is total less between groups i.e. a value of eighteen. In the fifth column, we have the mean Square Values (*MS*) which is calculated by dividing *SS* by the corresponding *df*. The sixth column is the *F statistic* which is the key statistic where we divide the *MS* between groups by the *MS* within group. Since our *F statistic* got a result 0.127 which is smaller than our *F-critical* value (8th column), this implies that we accept the H_0 i.e.

that all means are equal and reject H_1. Also, by analyzing that the *P-value* (7th column) which is 0.726 i.e. it is greater than the alpha value of 0.05, so we can also accept H_0 and reject H_1. The latency section of Tables 2, 3 and 4 follow the same detailed description as above, where we accept H_0 for all of the above-mentioned tables.

In the following Table 5, we have performed a one-way ANOVA which is based on our independent variable with four levels/groups (*M0*, *M30*, *M60*, and *M90*) for our dependent variables (amplitude and latency). Table 5 follows the same detailed description as explained beforehand for Table 2. The results show that we accept the null hypothesis for both the amplitude and latency since the P-value was higher than the original alpha value of 0.05 and the F statistic was lower than the F Critical value.

Table 5. One-way ANOVA statistical analysis on Amplitude and Latency – *M0* versus *M30* versus *M60* versus *M90*.

	Source of Variation	SS	df	MS	F	P-value	F Crit
Amplitude	BG	1.334	3	0.445	0.488	0.693	2.866
	WG	32.797	36	0.911			
	Total	34.131	39				
Latency	BG	1537.625	3	512.542	0.863	0.469	2.867
	WG	21371.75	36	593.660			
	Total	22909.375	39				

In the following Table 6, we have performed a one-way ANOVA which is based on our independent variable with three levels/groups (*M30*, *M60*, and *M90*) i.e. we want to assess if there is a statistical significance between the actual distractions. Table 6 follows the same detailed description as explained beforehand for Table 2. The results show that we accept the null hypothesis for both the amplitude and latency since the P-value was higher than the original alpha value of 0.05. This implies that there is no statistical significance between distractions.

Table 6. One-way ANOVA statistical analysis on Amplitude and Latency – *M30* versus *M60* versus *M90*.

	Source of Variation	SS	df	MS	F	P-value	F Crit
Amplitude	BG	1.320	2	0.660	0.851	0.438	3.354
	WG	20.931	27	0.775			
	Total	22.251	29				
Latency	BG	46.55	2	23.275	0.041	0.960	3.354
	WG	15215.025	27	563.519			
	Total	15261.575	29				

Table 7 shows the means for the dependent variables, amplitude and latency respectively according to levels of the independent variable rounded to the nearest hundredth. This data includes the average of all eight recorded electrodes throughout the five symbols and is shown per subject. Descriptive analysis shows that the highest amplitude was in the *M60* and the lowest amplitude was in the *M30*. On the other hand, the lowest latency was found in the *M60*, while the highest latency was found in the *M0*.

Table 7. Means and Standard Deviations (in Parentheses) for Amplitude (μV) & Latency (*ms*).

S	M0		M30		M60		M90	
	(μV)	*(ms)*	*(μV)*	*(ms)*	*(μV)*	*(ms)*	*(μV)*	*(ms)*
S1	4.90 (0.50)	466.5 (2.97)	2.09 (0.28)	473.5 (12.46)	3.90 (0.40)	470.5 (5.21)	2.88 (0.40)	462.5 (19.00)
S2	2.39 (1.14)	437.0 (82.16)	3.24 (0.35)	434.0 (76.58)	4.26 (0.41)	419.5 (54.15)	3.66 (0.83)	416 (66.69)
S3	3.29 (1.68)	431.0 (83.52)	2.18 (2.24)	417.0 (71.61)	4.03 (0.99)	430.0 (85.68)	3.64 (1.42)	423 (78.49)
S4	3.70 (0.98)	466.0 (107.5)	4.95 (0.54)	427.0 (82.11)	4.14 (0.45)	432.5 (86.76)	3.25 (1.08)	419.5 (75.49)
S5	3.96 (0.78)	444.0 (91.49)	4.11 (0.95)	431.0 (84.58)	4.61 (0.76)	428.5 (80.21)	4.77 (1.17)	436.5 (85.56)
S6	5.39 (1.64)	483.0 (1.85)	3.63 (2.44)	479.0 (17.73)	4.99 (2.40)	484.5 (3.96)	3.70 (2.12)	495 (2.83)
S7	1.70 (1.66)	430.5 (81.75)	4.94 (1.26)	431.5 (84.97)	4.18 (1.24)	427.5 (79.81)	4.58 (1.34)	449.5 (93.64)
S8	2.64 (1.38)	415.0 (71.10)	2.51 (1.57)	440.0 (72.88)	3.52 (1.22)	415.5 (66.91)	2.18 (1.69)	446.0 (90.16)
S9	4.46 (1.94)	439.0 (85.89)	2.50 (1.40)	415.5 (71.66)	2.17 (2.05)	424.0 (76.67)	3.67 (1.89)	411.0 (75.46)
S10	3.58 (0.26)	497.5 (87.40)	4.08 (0.71)	420.5 (80.61)	3.46 (0.61)	420.5 (76.98)	3.51 (0.46)	424.5 (84.43)
Avg	3.60 (1.83)	451.0 (69.56)	3.43 (1.66)	436.9 (65.52)	3.93 (1.38)	435.3 (61.63)	3.59 (1.46)	438.4 (67.18)

3.3 User Preference

Immediately after finishing the experiments, each subject was asked to participate in two voluntary questionnaires, to specify there preferred usage condition. The ranking consisted of a maximum weight value of four as the most desired and minimum weight value of one for the least desired. All ten subjects accepted to partake in the questionnaires. In the first questionnaire, (a) the subjects were allowed to give the same ranking to each independent variable, while (b) the subjects were asked to give a unique ranking to each independent variable.

In questionnaire (a) depicted in Table 8, the results show that as expected the *M0* independent variable got the highest ranking, followed by *M90*, *M60*, and *M30* respectively. The frequency analysis shows that *M0* got 100%, followed by *M90* with 87.5%, *M60* with 85%, and *M30* with 80%. It is noteworthy that the difference between *M0* and the second classified *M90* amounts to 12.5%, while when comparing *M90* i.e. the second place to the last-placed *M30* the difference was only 7.5%.

Table 8. User Preference for the questionnaire (a) allowing the same ranking and questionnaire (b) unique ranking.

S	M0		M30		M60		M90	
	(a)	(b)	(a)	(b)	(a)	(b)	(a)	(b)
S1	4	4	3	2	3	1	4	3
S2	4	4	4	3	3	1	3	2
S3	4	4	3	1	3	3	3	2
S4	4	4	3	1	3	2	4	3
S5	4	4	4	3	4	2	3	1
S6	4	4	4	1	4	3	4	2
S7	4	4	4	1	4	2	4	3
S8	4	4	2	1	3	2	3	3
S9	4	4	2	1	3	3	4	2
S10	4	4	3	1	4	3	3	2
Total	40/40	40/40	32/40	15/40	34/40	22/40	35/40	23/40
%	100	100	80	37.5	85	55	87.5	57.5

In questionnaire (b) depicted in the same Table 8, the results show that again as expected the *M0* independent variable had the maximum ranking, followed by *M90*, *M60*, and lastly *M30*. The frequency analysis shows that *M0* got 100%, followed by *M90* at 57.5%, *M60* at 55%, lastly *M30* at 37.5%. Once again, it is significant to note that the difference between *M0* and the second classified *M90* amounts to 42.5% and was the highest difference, even when comparing *M90* i.e. the second place to the last-placed *M30*, where the difference was 20%.

These results provide an overwhelming indication that the subjects preferred doing the experiments in a quiet setting, as was originally expected.

4 Conclusion

In direct continuation of our previous paper [3], this work analyzed the effect auditory distractions, explicitly those listed in our independent variables i.e. music at 0% - lab condition, music at 30%, music at 60%, and music at 90% have on the online performance i.e. accuracy, the offline performance i.e. latency and amplitude, and user preference, as expounded in the dependent variables. We enlisted ten healthy participants, who performed the aforementioned independent variables settings while making use of low-cost equipment. In addition, the research method for this study includes the use of Farwell & Donchin visual P300 speller based on the oddball paradigm in conjunction with the xDAWN algorithm.

The goal of our study is to develop a taxonomy aimed at categorizing distractions in the P300b domain and the effect that these distractions have on the success rate and signal characteristic i.e. amplitude, latency and signal morphology. This should give an overview on the viability and feasibility of the aforementioned P300 speller methodology and equipment to be utilized in the real-world environment. The aim of this paper was to analyze the effects that the aforementioned auditory distractions had on our dependent variables.

The null hypothesis based on our previous work [3] was that the distractions introduced in this study i.e. the independent variables, do not have a statistical significance effect on the dependent variables i.e. amplitude and latency. Statistical results for three, one-way ANOVA show that the null hypothesis was accepted for both amplitude and latency, as depicted from Tables 2, 3 and 4. Similarly, the results for the combined four levels/groups (*M0*, *M30*, *M60*, and *M90*), show that the null hypothesis was accepted for the amplitude and latency, as portrayed in Table 5. Analogously, the results for the combined three levels/groups between distractions i.e. *M30*, *M60*, and *M90*, do not show any statistical significance in both amplitude and latency and hence the null hypothesis was accepted as well, as represented in Table 6.

Descriptive results for the dependent variables show that (1) the accuracy was maximum at the *M0* with 100%, followed unexpectedly by *M90* at 98%, and shadowed equally by *M60* and *M30* at 96%, as portrayed in Table 1, (2) the amplitude was maximal at the *M60* with 3.93 μV, shadowed by *M0* with 3.60 μV, *M90* with 3.59 μV, and *M30* with 3.43 μV as portrayed in Table 7, (3) the latency was lowest at the *M60*, shadowed by *M30*, *M90*, and *M0*, likewise portrayed in Table 7.

The user preference questionnaire as portrayed in Table 8, (a) show overwhelmingly that subjects preferred the *M0* condition as originally expected, trailed surprisingly by *M90*, *M60*, and *M30*, and questionnaire (b) subjects chose anew the *M0*, shadowed by *M90*, *M60*, and lastly by *M30*.

In this work, the introduction of an extendable hierarchical taxonomy aimed at categorizing distractions in the P300b domain was introduced, as depicted in Fig. 1. Explicitly, the effect that the aforementioned independent variables, categorized under auditory distractions, have on the dependent variables. In the future, we plan to introduce additional types of distractions which are commonly found in a real-world environment and include it within the different categories of our taxonomy .

References

1. Schembri, P., Pelc, M., Ma, J.: Comparison between a passive and active response task and their effect on the amplitude and latency of the P300 component for visual stimuli while using low fidelity equipment. In: Forty First Annual International Conference of the IEEE Engineering in Medicine and Biology Society, EMBC 2019 (2019)
2. Schembri, P., Pelc, M., Ma, J.: Impact of mental fatigue during repetitive exercises of a visual P300 speller. In: 13th International Conference on Bio-Inspired Systems and Singal Processing - BIOSTEC BIOSIGNALS (2020)
3. Schemrbi, P., Pelc, M. and Ma, J.: The effect that an auditory distraction with differing levels of intensity have on a visual P300 speller while utilizing low fidelity equipment: alongside the development of a taxonomy. In: Proceedings of the 3rd International Conference on Computer-Human Interaction Research and Applications - Volume 1: CHIRA, pp. 50–58 (2019). https://doi.org/10.5220/0008065200500058. ISBN 978-989-758-376-6, ISSN 2184-3244
4. Schembri, P., Pelc, M., Ma, J.: The effect that auxiliary taxonomized auditory distractions have on a P300 speller while utilising low fidelity equipment. In: 11th Computer Science and Electronic Engineering Conference (CEEC 2019) (2019)
5. Kam, J.W., Griffin, S., Shen, A., Patel, S., Hinrichs, H., Heinze, H.-J., Deouell, L.Y., Knight, R.T.: Systematic comparison between a wireless EEG system with dry electrodes and a wired EEG system with wet electrodes. NeuroImage **184**(1), 119–129 (2019)
6. Bradford, C.J., Burke, B., Nguyen, C., Slipher, G.A., Mrozek, R., Hairston, D.: Performance of conformable, dry EEG sensors. In: 40th Annual International Conference of the IEEE Engineering in Medicine and Biology Society (EMBC), pp. 4957–4960 (2018)
7. Nam, C.S., Li, Y., Johnson, S.: Evaluation of P300-based brain-computer interface in real-world contexts. Int. J. Hum. Comput. Inter. **26**(6), 621–637 (2010)
8. Valentin, O., Ducharme, M., Cretot-Richert, G., Monsarrat-Chanon, H., Viallet, G., Delnavaz, A., Voix, J.: Validation and benchmarking of a wearable EEG acquisition platform for real-world applications. IEEE Trans. Biomed. Circuits Syst. **13**(1), 103–111 (2019)
9. Zink, R., Hunyadi, B., Huffel, S.V., Vos, M.D.: Mobile EEG on the bike: disentangling attentional and physical contributions to auditory attention tasks. J. Neural Eng. **13**(4), 046017 (2016)
10. Oliveira, A.S., Schlink, B.R., Hairston, D.W., König, P., Ferris, D.P.: Proposing metrics for benchmarking novel EEG technologies towards real-world measurements. Front. Hum. Neurosci. **10**, 188 (2016)
11. Farwell, L.A., Donchin, E.: Talking off the top of your head: toward a mental prosthesis utilizing event-related brain potentials. Electroencephalography Clin. Neurophysiol. **70**, 510–523 (1988)
12. Rivet, B., Souloumiac, A., Attina, V., Gibert, G.: xDAWN algorithm to enhance evoked potentials: application to brain-computer interface. IEEE Trans. Biomed. Eng. **56**(8), 2035–2043 (2009)
13. Woehrle, H., Krell, M.M., Straube, S., Kim, S.K., Kirchner, E.A., Kirchner, F.: An adaptive spatial filter for user-independent single trial detection of event-related potentials. IEEE Trans. Biomed. Eng. **62**(7), 1696–1705 (2015)
14. Clerc, M., Bougrain, L., Lotte, F., (eds.) Brain Computer Interfaces 2 - Technology and Applications. Wiley (2016)

Author Index

Printed in the United States
By Bookmasters